Climbing
the
Money Mountain

Randy Loren

Climbing the Money Mountain

Copyright © 2007 by Randy Loren

Published by Financial Nation Publications,

a division of Financial Nation, Inc., Lighthouse Point, Florida.

ATTENTION: SCHOOLS AND UNIVERSITIES

Quantity discounts are available for purchase
for educational purposes from
Financial Nation Publications
by calling 954-234-3962
or emailing randy@randyloren.com

Visit us on the worldwide web at
http://www.RandyLoren.com

Library of Congress Control Number: 2007935159
ISBN: 978-0-9797636-0-1 (Soft Cover Edition)
ISBN: 978-0-9797636-1-8 (Hard Cover Edition)

Printed in the United States of America
10 9 8 7 6 5 4 3 2 1

I dedicate this book…

To my daughters, Mandy and Ally, *"Climbing the Money Mountain,"* is my gift to you.

To my wife Beth, who for twenty five years has supported me whenever I wanted to tackle another goal in my life, no matter how the odds were stacked against me.

To Patti Smith for her tremendous help in editing and offering feedback as I wrote this book, and for her incredible insight into business and global issues. Patti is truly one of the most gifted writers and well-read individuals that I have ever met. I look forward to her participation in future projects.

To high school students and all young adults…*never give up on your dreams.* Dreams are the beginning of imagination, creativity and innovation. With dreams come goals, accomplishments, and the opportunity to make what once seemed impossible… *possible.*

Introduction

Climbing the Money Mountain was written for you, an extremely eager young adult, who is full of potential with a whole life of exciting and wonderful times ahead of you. You may not have realized it yet, but your future can be anything you want it to be. You could become the next great statesman or the Einstein of your generation. Perhaps you will be the one to find the cure for cancer. Maybe you will be the best doctor, lawyer, or business leader the world has ever known. Or just maybe you aspire to be a great mother, a loving father, and/or a good husband or wife.

You truly have so much ahead of you at this point in your life. It is now up to you to make your life the best you can. It is your life, and you can achieve all the goals you set forth as you embark on the exciting journey that lies ahead. Take a cue from George Bailey…*Jimmy Stewart's character in the holiday cult movie classic, "It's a Wonderful Life", an old movie from your grandparent's generation that is resurrected every Christmas and shown on television many times a day during the holiday season.* In this great old movie, George Bailey learns that what is best and most worthwhile in life can't be bought in a store or earned on Wall Street. It is not what we own that makes our lives worthy. It is who we are, who we choose to bring into our lives, and how we affect the lives of those closest to us, which will bring the greatest rewards in life. The rest is just window dressing in our material world.

The future is yours. Never let anyone tell you differently. It does not matter whether you are the sharpest wit in your class or one of the most challenged. What matters is that you want to work hard, and learn from the wisdom and the talents of those you meet along the way, who can help you to be better today than you were yesterday.

I wrote this book as help and guidance for my children, Mandy and Ally, when they were both teenagers with their whole adult life of great opportunity and adventures ahead of them. I wanted them to be aware of a few things I had learned that could create frustration and great anxiety in their lives if they were not careful. Both of my girls told me that there was a chance this book could be a help to their friends, and maybe even every teenager or young adult getting ready to go out into the world on their own. Hopefully, they were right and I can help you learn about some of the stumbling blocks life has to put in your path. There are more than a few financial obstacles that you need to be aware of, and hopefully avoid, and many personal choices you will need to make as you climb up your money mountain. I know that you will discover in this financial and personal guide book, just enough information to get you on the right track, so you can avoid these troubling obstacles, making your climb to the top of your money mountain easier, and your journey less treacherous.

Table of Contents

The Money Mountain

Chapter

"Believe you can and you're halfway there"

Theodore Roosevelt

You're 18 years old, on top of the world, about to graduate high school, and counting the days until you're in control of your life and away from Mom and Dad's rules. No curfews, no one to tell you what to do, on your way to college, trade school or maybe that first post high school job. No parent bugging you, with questions like, *"Did you do your homework?"*… *"Did you brush your teeth?"*… *"Did you clean your room?"*… *"What time will you be home?"*… *"Where are you going and with whom?"* You're thinking: *"It's my life! And soon I'll be the one in complete control of it."*

Sounds great to you, doesn't it? But along with this new-found freedom comes some uncharted waters. There have been some before you who were able to dive right in and swim with ease. However, too many find themselves merely treading water throughout their entire lifetime, struggling just to keep their head above the ever-changing and unpredictable seas, hoping to avoid sinking to the bottom.

Most all teenagers feel invincible as they approach the end of their high school years. Life on your own terms sounds so good, and it can be really great, but one of the first lessons that most of us learn is that nothing is as simple as you think it will be. The good news is that there is a secret to financial success and the sooner you learn the lessons of money, the better off you will be.

By using the tools of proper financial planning and learning to make the right choices, the goals you set for these "money chapters" of your life often will be easily accomplished and may well surpass even your wildest dreams. These money decisions, whether big or small, will impact you in a big way. It's up to you whether the outcome of your decisions will help you climb higher up the money mountain or whether you will stumble and begin to fall.

Have you ever wondered how people become successful and accumulate wealth? We have all heard the success stories of professional athletes, like golf sensation Tiger Woods who earns millions of dollars a year, or an actress, like Cameron Diaz, who makes millions of dollars per movie. As we grow up, we all dream about being rich and famous just like them. They made it look easy to reach the pinnacle of success in their professions but if you were to ask, they would tell you that acquiring professional success takes hard work. They would also tell you that staying at the peak and holding on to the wealth of your money mountain takes being smart about money and knowing how money works.

Business icons like real estate billionaire Donald Trump, whose name is recognized by some 98% of Americans according to a Gallup poll, has worked hard to climb up his money mountain, but even Donald Trump nearly fell from the peak. His fortune was almost wiped out when billions of dollars of real estate loans came due and he was unable to make the payment. Trump was determined to regain his reputation and to keep his wealth. He worked even harder to remain at the peak of his money mountain by using his business smarts and recognized name to regain his fortune. As host of the television show *"The Apprentice,"* he is known to millions of Americans thanks in part to his trademark phrase, *"You're fired!"* Today, he is richer and wiser. He has diversified his money mountain to include television, publishing, fashion, and financial services, to name just a few of his business interests, as a complement to his real estate empire.

Another example of someone who took a different path to the top of his mountain is renowned scientist and author Stephen Hawking, who many say is one of the greatest scientists the world has known. Professor Hawking, who authored the best-selling book "A Brief History of Time", worked on the basic laws which govern the universe. He showed that Albert Einstein's General Theory of Relativity implied that space and time have a beginning, in the Big Bang, and an end, in Black Holes. What makes Hawking so great is not only his genius that has allowed him to solve questions others throughout history have been unable to solve, but in the face of a debilitating and deadly disease, he has continued his work. ALS, or amyotrophic lateral sclerosis which is a motor neuron disease, stripped his body of all motor functions and caused him to need 24 hour a day nursing care, but still he continued moving forward and teaching mathematics at the University of Cambridge. Even today he continues to conduct research, write articles and books, and speeches.

In 2007, Professor Hawking boarded a specially equipped Boeing 727 that transported him into the sky to create a Zero-Gravity like experience. *"It was amazing…I could have gone on and on. Space, here I come."* said Hawking speaking through his voice-synthesized computer. This is important because, even though this terrible disease robbed him of motor functions like feeding himself and speaking without the aid of a machine, he never gave up climbing his mountain, even when his body gave up on him.

Oprah Winfrey, another household name, had to overcome many adversities growing up, including childhood abuse, to reach her mountain's peak. Even though life in her early years was at times tough and cruel, she never gave up, and for the last quarter century has been one of the most successful TV personalities in America. She was recognized in 2003 as the first African American woman to be named a billionaire by Forbes magazine. Over the years, she has given countless millions of dollars to charities around the world and has helped innumerable people through her generous donations.

Most of these people, you have probably heard of, but there are many millions of people that you never hear of, who have worked hard every day of their lives, striving to reach the peak of their own stupendous money mountain. Everyday people, that you will never meet or hear anything about, will reach the top of their mountain's crest. Each one of these people had different goals, and each followed different paths on their journey. Each journey probably took years of hard work, a little luck, and even major setbacks along the way that they had to overcome.

The one thing, each of these successful people has in common, is that they never gave up, and they always found a way to hold their head high even in the most difficult of situations.

This book is called *"Climbing the Money Mountain"* because every man and woman needs to understand the **Basics of Money:** *how to earn it, how to keep it and how to see it grow.* Even if great wealth is not one of your goals, you will undoubtedly be living in a society where money is used as a medium of exchange for all your needs and creature comforts. Whether you become rich in monetary terms, or rich only in your heart, this book will help you think about your own ambitions and how to avoid obstacles that could keep you from reaching your goals.

So, get ready to take your first steps climbing up your money mountain. You will learn how to plan so that you will be able to make your journey to your mountain's peak, and fulfill the dreams and aspirations of the bright and prosperous future that you deserve.

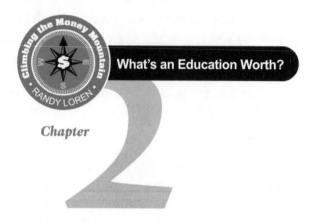

*"An Investment in Knowledge Pays
the Best Interest"*

Benjamin Franklin

Take a moment to think about what it would be like to climb Mount Everest from its base to its summit. First, it is over 29,000 feet high. It has unforgiving extremes in temperatures and oxygen levels. At the base of Mount Everest, on a clear day, you can stand and breathe easily while gazing up the mountain to its beautiful snow-covered top.

But at the top of the mountain, you could not breathe without the right equipment and your limbs would freeze very quickly without the proper protective clothing. In fact, the temperature at the top can be as low as 76° below zero in the midst of winter. Fierce winds and sand storms can come upon you un-expectedly, some with winds clocked as high as 177 miles per hour. Unsuspecting mountain climbers have been hit by bliz-zards dropping as much as 10 feet of snow that came, seem-ingly, out of nowhere.

Without notice, mountain paths can become blocked, leaving no way out. Avalanches are the main cause of death on this mountain even for the most experienced of climbers. For ev-ery 50 successful climbs to the summit, one climber will die.

To climb Mount Everest to its peak and return to tell about it, you must be prepared, not only for what is expected, but for what is not expected. Though, for the few that have reached the highest point of Mount Everest, they say it is an incredible journey, and a wonderful, life-changing accomplishment.

Climbing up the Money Mountain in your life will at times be difficult. Successful people know that good outcomes in life require work, and the climb up your money mountain will be similar to climbing a real mountain like Mount Everest. You will encounter the expected and the unexpected. At times you will stumble and fall, only to have to pull yourself up and look for another path to the top. The good news is that when you arrive at the top of your Money Mountain, you will know it, and you will be proud that you succeeded in following your own path to the top.

Your climb up the Money Mountain will be a series of steps. Each step, when mastered, takes you a little closer to your mountain's peak. The first step of your expedition to the top begins at the base of the mountain and is known as the **Education Step.** The Education Step is defined by the amount of higher education you will need to enter the profession you choose to pursue. Whether it is High School, College, or Post College Study, your decision will probably impact your money future. You have been told by teachers, parents and researchers to stay in school and graduate and they were right.

The more education you complete, the more money you can earn, and the more career options you will have during your lifetime.

Think about this question. *Have you personally known someone who did not finish High School?* If so, do you know where they are today? Odds are, if you do know someone who dropped out of high school, they are like most other high school dropouts: struggling to pay their monthly living expenses, in a dead end job, and likely wishing they had stayed in school.

Success stories of high school dropouts who achieved a high degree of success in business and made large sums of money are very few and far between. The vast majority of success stories are of people who acquired wealth after finishing school, and then continued learning throughout their career. Dave Thomas of Wendy's Restaurant fame is one of a very few who was extremely successful in business, even though he did not earn a high school diploma as a teenager. Thomas knew that his business and financial success in life was rare for someone with almost no formal education. In his later years, he worried that his amazing business success might give teenagers the wrong impression about the importance of an education, so he went back to high school to earn his GED.

Dave Thomas' desire to help others understand the importance of a good education caused him to support the "Enterprise Ambassador Program" in the State of Florida. This unique program provides high school students the opportunity to learn about the Free Enterprise System through their school's business education program. Thanks to this mentoring program, students are able to discuss real-life business situations, one-on-one with a successful member of the business community, so they can increase their understanding of the business and financial world. Dave Thomas once said, "Get all the education you can. Who knows what I could have achieved if I'd stayed in school and went to college? The possibilities are endless when you have an education."

Think about this question.

If you had a child, would you want your child to earn a high school degree and go on to college or vocational school, or would you like your child to be a high school dropout with very little hope for a bright financial future?

The human spirit says we want our children to do better than we did. You often see bumper stickers that proudly proclaim *"My Child made the Honor Roll at ABC High School"*. Did you ever see a bumper sticker that read *"My Child is a High School Dropout"?* Let face it, most everybody would prefer to earn a good wage that will buy them a beautiful home of their own and a nice car parked in their garage. Few long to work for minimum wage, while they live with friends in a rented home, and drive an old broken down car with no extra money to spend on fun and a few of life's luxuries.

The key to a bright financial future is to get a good education, work hard, and be rewarded for your efforts.

Sometimes your reward will come in the form of monetary compensation, but sometimes your reward will come as nothing more than just a good old pat on the back from a parent, a teacher or your boss. Some of you may see these simple rewards as worthless, but rest assured, sincere praise for a job well done can impact you in very positive ways and influence the choices you will make in the future.

Let's look at the facts. In Figure 1 on the next page, individual median annual incomes are compared at different levels of completed education.

Median Annual Income
By Highest Level of Education
National Center for Education Statistics (2004) Figure 1

Some High School - No Completion	High School Completion	Associates Degree	Bachelor's Degree	Masters Degree	Doctorate Degree
$26,277	$35,725	$44,404	$57,220	$71,530	$82,401

As you can see from the chart above; a person with a high school education earns $9,448 a year more than someone who does not complete high school; and, a person with a four-year college degree earns $30,943 a year more than someone who does not earn their high school diploma. *Which group would you like to join?*

The facts are simple:

> *The more education you complete,*
> *the more income you will earn.*

When you're young, it's hard to understand the importance of a solid educational foundation for your future. Many young people today complain about going to school and say "School is so boring", while other students love school and want more. The facts are that, if you don't finish high school, you will lose a lot of money over your lifetime. So, use your education to your benefit. Finish high school, then go to vocational school or college, and constantly absorb information.

According to the United States Department of Labor, people between the ages 18-40 will have 10.5 jobs during this time in their lives. *The data also shows that the less education a person has the more often they will be unemployed during this period.* That means, those teenagers who choose not to graduate from high school will on average be unemployed far more often than those who do the smart thing and complete their high school education.

So, if you want to greatly improve your odds of getting and keeping a good job, stay in school and get as much education as you can.

When you finally graduate and move into the job market, you should:

- Continue adding to your knowledge base by reading books and periodicals, like trade journals for example, that will help you to stay on top of how the business world is changing. Attend seminars to improve on your skills and to learn new skills that will help you better perform in your job.

- Develop mentor relationships with people in your profession so that you may learn from them how to be better at your profession.

This dedication to learning throughout your lifetime will help you to prepare yourself for the continually changing world of business that will undoubtedly impact your profession and your financial future.

Bank Checking Accounts

Chapter 3

"*The gratification of wealth is not found in mere possessions or in lavish expenditures but in its wise application.*"

Miguel de Cervantes

As you near the end of your high school career you should, if you have not already done so, establish a business relationship with a financial institution such as a bank. Whether you go to college, or go directly into the workplace, you will need supplies for everyday life, like food and clothes. You will need to pay bills when they come due, like your electric bill, cell phone, cable and rent, just to name a few.

This business relationship that you begin with a bank will be, for most young people, the first step up the money mountain.

How you handle this new relationship will, to a great extent, determine your financial future.

Do a good job of managing your bank relationship and it can help set you on the right path up the mountain. Do a bad job of managing your bank relationship by spending money you don't have, or making late payments on a loan, and you will damage your relationship with the bank.

Write a few bad checks, even by accident, and you may well block or significantly alter your path up the money mountain. One of the first things you need to learn about banks is that they have a long memory and they share news of how you manage your bank relationship with other banks.

The most basic of all bank products is a checking account. A checking account gives you the ability to put your money in a safe place, so you can buy items you need and pay your bills with the money you keep in the bank. When you go to open your new bank account, an employee of the bank will normally ask for two pieces of identification — one with a picture on it like a driver's license, and another form of identification such as a social security card. The bank will then issue you a checkbook.

You may write checks only up to the amount of money, *or funds*, you have in your checking account. You may deposit and withdraw money at any time, as long as you do not try to withdraw more money than you have available in your account. Writing a check that is not backed up by money in your account is often called "bouncing a check" because, when the check is submitted to your bank for payment, it bounces back to the person to whom you wrote the check. Not only is knowingly writing bad checks against the law, it can be a very negative influence on your climb up the money mountain.

The bank may also provide you with a debit card which gives

you the option of making purchases at stores using this card instead of a writing a check. It is often easier to make a purchase in a store with a debit card, but you must remember to make note in your check registry of purchases made with your debit card, because those funds are coming directly out of your checking account just as if you were writing a check.

FACTS ABOUT DEBIT CARDS:

A debit card is NOT like a credit card, even though they may look the same and both display a VISA or MasterCard logo. When you use a credit card, the bank loans you money to pay back later with interest. A debit card, even though the word VISA appears on the card, immediately reduces your bank balance, even faster than writing a check.

Here is an example of a problem that was created by a debit card holder, who did not thoroughly understand the difference between a debit card and credit card. The debit card holder had opened a new checking account at a local bank branch. The bank officer who opened his account issued him a Visa Debit Card, saying that the card "could be used at most all stores and restaurants." The most important fact that the bank officer did not make clear to this young inexperienced bank customer was: when you use the debit card, the money is immediately withdrawn from your checking account. It is NOT treated like a regular credit card transaction which is repaid at a later date when your monthly statement arrives in the mail. As a result, he incurred over $350 in overdraft fees.

A debit card can only be used up to the amount of funds you have in your bank account, and no more. Otherwise, you may overdraft your account and incur extremely high overdraft fees.

Here is how a checking account works:

Let's say you open a checking account at the bank with a deposit of $200 in cash and that becomes your opening balance. Next, you go to a department store and purchase items totaling $25, and you pay for them by writing a check. You will now have $175 left in your checking account.

When you write a check, you should always immediately write the amount of the check in your checkbook's registry.

If you don't write it in the registry when you write the check, you might forget, and later think your available funds are more than the money you actually have left in your account. That's one of the easiest ways to accidentally bounce a check.

You never want to write a check for more than you have in your account because the check will not be honored by your bank, and you will be charged an Insufficient Funds Fee. That bank fee will probably cost you $35, or possibly much more. *If you write bad checks often, your bank might decide that you do not manage your money well. That is when the bank will limit your ability to do future business with the bank.*

If you immediately note the amount of a check or debit charge in your check registry, you will greatly reduce the chance of getting on the wrong side of your bank, just because you didn't know your current checking account balance. Most banks today offer online banking, which makes it possible for you to view your current and past bank account information on the Internet, 24 hours a day. Online banking is a good way to double-check your registry without waiting for your monthly bank statement.

AVOID CASH CHECKING STORES

Instead of setting up a bank account, some people use check-cashing stores to do their banking business. A check-cashing store will allow you to cash an employer payroll check or a check given to you by a friend, but the problem is they charge

VERY HIGH FEES to cash your check.

If you cash a payroll check at a check-cashing store, you will automatically be earning less than you thought for your hard work because of the fee you have to pay to cash your check.

Today, some banks will actually charge a fee to cash a check, written from their own bank, if you don't have an account at that bank. *You work hard for your money and having a checking account will help you avoid the need to use a check-cashing store.* It is much better for you to open your own checking account, and maintain your account responsibly, so you will be able to simply deposit your pay check and get the cash you need.

If you establish a banking relationship with a nationwide financial institution, like Bank of America, Washington Mutual, Wachovia, or Citibank to name a few, you have an outlet to write checks, use an Automatic Teller Machine (ATM), or make deposits at locations all across the country. Many community banks and credit unions may even waive ATM fees when using another bank's ATM. Research the banks, and the benefits of the checking products they offer, before opening an account. Make a list of the services you will need, and then choose the bank that will meet your needs, at the least cost to you.

Top Six Things to Consider When Choosing a Bank

1. Many banks today do not charge a monthly fee for maintaining an account relationship, while others charge a high monthly fee for the account. Form your banking relationship with a bank that does not charge you for maintaining a checking account.

2. When researching banks, be sure to ask the bank's representative if they hold the checks that you deposit for

several days. If they do hold the checks you deposit, then your money will not be available to you until after the hold is released. Ask the bank representative if it is possible to take the hold off checks you deposit to your account. If they say "No", talk to another bank.

3. Some banks will charge a fee for the privilege of using their debit card, however, NO MONTHLY FEE debit cards are available.

4. Some banks charge very high fees for ATM transactions and some charge nothing for ATM transactions. If there is any charge for using their ATM machines, or other ATM machines owned by other banks or institutions, know the fees per transaction. These fees can add up very quickly and become an unexpected, hidden expense that can cost you a lot every month.

5. Bank employees are often compensated in some way to open new accounts and attract new customers. They will want to help you more if you look professional and present yourself in a professional manner.

6. Let the bank representative assisting you know that this process is all new to you. Make it clear to them that you hope to build a long term bank relationship with their bank so that, when you get ready to buy a car and your first home, you will have a trusted financial relationship to count on.

Do not be afraid to tell the bank representative what you want from your banking partner. They may be able to offer you more than you think. They may have the ability to waive fees, remove the fund hold periods, eliminate ATM fees, if any, and to offer you an incentive gift for opening an account at their bank. If you're a student, they may have a special student checking account product just perfect for you. Ask questions.

They want to help you. Remember, you are the customer. Let them know that you could go to any bank for a checking account, but you chose to go with them. When you're in front of the bank employee, you must show them that you are very confident, professional, and you will make a great new client for their bank. The bottom line is that the bank will be lucky to have you.

Another very important option, that you might want to consider when setting up your checking account, is opening a savings account, too. Opening a savings account at the same bank means that the two accounts can be tied together so you can easily transfer money from your checking into your savings account. Even if you can save only a little money each month, the dollars add up over time, and when that first big purchase comes up, a healthy savings account could be the difference between being approved for a loan and being rejected.

When you learn to use all the traditional and the newer electronic forms of bank transactions, you probably won't be writing that many paper checks. If you maintain your checking account responsibly and keep up a good relationship with your bank, you will have many different and advantageous types of financial transactions available to you. Debit cards, credit cards, online bill pay, online transfers, and even cash will help to make your financial life easier to manage, but opening a checking account is a very important and big first step in securing your financial future.

Chapter

Credit

"While we are free to choose our actions, we are not free to choose the consequences of our actions."

Stephen R. Covey

The Responsibility of Credit Cards

There was a time in America, when it was very difficult to get credit. Most of America used to be, pretty much, Cash & Carry only. Today, however, our society is running rampant with fast and loose credit offers, coming at you from every direction. It is very easy to unintentionally overspend, and quickly get into serious financial trouble, if you haven't done the proper planning.

Beware of easy credit. The easy credit standard that exists in America today has created a society of borrowers. As of May 2007, American consumers were estimated to carry 2.4 trillion dollars in debt, according to the Federal Reserve. That is not good for you, nor is it good for the country.

More and more often, American consumers are finding that they are not able to pay back money they borrowed on credit, and dealing with the banks and other lenders has become far more difficult.

The 2007 credit crunch, which was created in part by loose lending standards and home values appreciating at an unprecedented rate, followed by a decline in Real Estate values, created a country of borrowers. It is estimated that up to 2 million homeowners could lose their home to foreclosure, while many others may survive a foreclosure but find that they are left with a damaged credit history due to over borrowing on credit cards so they could pay their mortgage. Compound this with the fact that credit card companies can change the rules of your business arrangement at any time they like, in any way they like, and things may get worse, before they get better. Thanks to virtually no government regulation of the credit card industry, these money lenders can dramatically increase your interest rate, if you are just a few days late with a payment. And when you get behind in your payments, you will find yourself quickly getting further and further behind, thanks to higher interest rates and sky high late fees. Not being able to pay back your debt is something you want to avoid as you climb your money mountain.

The next step up the mountain will be to fully understand the concept of credit. Perhaps, as you finish high school and most certainly as you enter college, credit card companies like Discover, MasterCard and Visa will be offering you a brand new credit card of your very own.

As you were growing up, you probably watched your parents use their credit cards to buy something for you at a local retail store. Did you ever wonder what happened after your parents used their credit card? If you were like most kids, you probably never thought about it at all. Most kids are more concerned about what their parents bought them than what happens after the sales clerk processes Mom or Dad's credit card. *Ah, the good old days of financial innocence.* Sadly, when you get your first credit card, your good old days of financial innocence are over.

Now is the time for you to fully and completely understand credit cards, and how this valuable knowledge can protect you and help you get closer to the top of your mountain.

Let's say you're starting college, and one of the large credit card companies offers you an application to acquire one of their credit cards with a $300 credit limit to start. Your initial reaction might be, "Wow, this is so cool. Now I can buy whatever I want just like my parents did!" To sweeten the deal the credit card company will issue the card with your new college logo imprinted on it. The typical reaction is "Where do I sign?" Though a credit card is something that most young adults want, it is important to understand just how this new-found freedom can impact your life. Without some careful understanding and planning, that credit card that once seemed like a dream come true, can quickly turn into your worst nightmare.

So let's take a close look at credit cards because they are one of the first steps in building your financial future.

A credit card looks like a simple piece of plastic but it is the beginning of your ability to buy what you need and what you want without using cash for the purchase. A credit card is very different from a debit card. With a credit card, the bank is extending to you a line of credit so that you may easily borrow money from the bank and you must repay this loan with interest. With a debit card, you are spending your money directly from your checking account which is decreased each time you make a purchase.

What you most need to understand about the concept of credit is that it can help you, but it can also hurt you very badly. Understanding credit early can help get you prepare for a great and rewarding future.

We'll start with wealth. Wealth is not only about how much money you have in the bank, it also is based on your ability to borrow money and pay it back. Let's look at an example. On March 1, you charge $110.00 on your new credit card to buy these really cool Nike running shoes you saw while tuning in to your favorite TV show. Three weeks after the purchase on March 22, you get a credit card bill from the bank that issued you the credit card. The statement lists the transaction for the shoe purchase and indicates that you can pay all of the $110.00 you owe or only a small portion of it, called the Minimum Payment Due, which is only $15.00 and is due by April 10.

Now, here is an important point to remember…

The credit card company will consider you a good customer, only if you:

1. send a check or pay the bill online,

2. pay at least the $15.00 minimum that is due, in this example , or any amount up to the total balanced owed of $110.00, and

3. as long as your payment is received by the due date of April 10.

If, however, your payment is received after April 10 but before the next statement date, then the credit card company will charge you a late fee which can be as high as $39 dollars or more.

If the worst should happen and your payment is not received before your next statement is mailed, you will not only be charged a late fee, along with the monthly interest charge, but you will also get a bad credit rating issued against you.

What makes this even worse is that your credit card company will notify all the credit information bureaus that you are a potential credit risk. Then the credit bureaus will report to all companies who might consider giving you credit in the future, that you have had a late payment and are a credit risk...*just because you didn't pay your bill on time.*

Another example of how you can easily destroy your credit rating is: you buy a new cell phone from a leading telecommunications company and you forget to pay your bill on time. Now you have another late payment showing on your credit report. Every time you make a late payment it may be reported to the credit bureaus. If you make too many late payments, the next time you try to get credit with a company they may say "No", just because you paid your bills a few days late.

The more late payments you have listed on your credit report, the more difficult it is going to be for you to obtain credit from other companies when you need it most.

It is also possible that the credit card companies you have been paying late may decide to close your account, so that you are most assuredly no longer able to use their credit card. Even if they choose not to close your account, they may raise your interest rate to a default rate of 20-25%, or higher. You may find that you will have difficulty making your payments, thanks to the greatly increased amounts of interest you will have to pay each and every month.

Late credit card accounts can lower your overall credit rating, as can be seen from the following example:

Let's say you need a new car and have been eyeing a particular make and model on the local auto lot. You sit down with the dealership's finance manager to buy the new car, but he tells you that your credit score is too low to give you the best finance rate. He says, as a result of late payments on your credit card bills, your credit rating has dropped and the bank he uses for financing believes that you are now a credit risk. The bank says they will lend you money to purchase the car, but you will have to put more upfront money towards the purchase and that your interest rate will be much higher.

They agree to lend you $20,000 towards the $25,000 purchase. Thus you have to put $5,000 down towards the purchase of the car.

It gets worse. At the time you are borrowing the money, the best car loan rate for the bank's best customers is 8%, spread out over 60 monthly payments. So, the monthly payment for your new car, assuming you have very good credit, would be $405.53.

But, if your credit report shows some late payments and your credit rating isn't very good, that increases the bank's risk on the loan and banks don't like increased risk. So there is only one way the bank will lend you money to purchase the car. You must pay for their increased risk. That means, that instead of paying 8% interest for 60 months, you will have to pay 14% interest for 60 months on the $20,000 you borrow. Your payments have just gone up $59.84 a month due to the fact that you have bad credit because you forget to pay your bills on time. *See figure 2 below.*

Figure 2	Interest Rate	Loan Amount	Monthly Payment	Total of Payments
Best Bank Customers	8%	$20,000.00	$405.53	$24,331.80
Bad Credit Customers	14%	$20,000.00	$465.37	$27,922.20

Over the 60 months you make payments on your new car, *the additional interest you will have to pay the bank will total $3,590.40.*

What could you have done with that extra $3,590.40? You could probably do something much better with it than helping the bank increase their profit margin.

The bottom line is: make sure you always pay your bills on time! It is an important step in getting the best interest rates and terms when you borrow money.

Now, let's discuss where companies go to find out about your credit rating. There are three credit repositories that hold all your credit information and they sell this information to companies that are considering extending you credit or giving you a loan.

The three credit repositories are known as Experian, Transunion, and Equifax.

Here is how the credit system works in America. Each time a company lets you borrow money, that company gives a credit report on your credit history to one or all of the repositories, and tells them how you did. Whether the loan is on a credit card, a car loan, a personal bank loan, or a home loan, all lenders issue reports about you to other credit agencies. Your past behavior follows you wherever you go for a long time.

Did you make payments on time in the full amount as agreed each month?

Did you pay off the entire amount owed to the creditor and satisfy the loan and the lender?

If you did, great! If you failed to make the minimum monthly payments, then you will be issued a late notice on your credit report for the entire business world to see.

Many people believe that these late payment entries on your credit report will go away, but they are mistaken. A bad credit rating will stay on your credit report for a very long time. Each time you pay late, your credit rating goes lower, and each time, your ability to borrow money in the future is reduced.

We will discuss more about credit in later chapters, but always remember…

Pay your credit cards ON TIME, and NEVER be late. If you cannot afford it and cannot pay for it, DO NOT BUY IT!!

You must always use your credit cards prudently and only when necessary. It is way too easy to borrow more money than you can afford to pay back, and it will get you in trouble, resulting in credit warnings being issued by the credit repository against you.

FACT: Not only will banks often not lend you money if you have bad credit, but an employer may decide not to offer you a job because they see that you have a bad credit report. They may believe that you are unstable, not reliable, and could be a risk to their organization. So keep your credit rating high by always paying your bills on time.

Chapter

College

Climbing the Money Mountain

RANDY LOREN

"Always dream and shoot higher than you know you can. Don't bother just to be better than your contemporaries or predecessors try to be better than yourself."

William Faulkner

Starting College or Vocational School

Have you ever known a parent, grandparent or friend who was absolutely obsessed about their college football team even though they finished college years ago? Every Saturday during college football season, past graduates watch their school's football game as if it were the last football game they would ever see. Even though they may now live thousands of miles away from where they went to college, all you have to do is just mention their old college football team to see a grown man or woman act like a little kid who just opened their first birthday present. They are their college's best recruiting force and will, for the rest of their lives, be their alma mater's most willing and loyal college cheerleaders.

College has that impact on many people. It's the time of life when we are nearing adulthood but still enjoy having fun like a child. It's also the time when you are going out on your own and you have to learn how to do all the things that Mom and Dad always did for you.

Now, you will have to wash your own clothes.

You will have to pay your own bills.

There will be no parents around to ask for that extra ten bucks you need to buy a late night pizza with friends.

No parent yelling from another room like a human alarm clock — *"Get out of bed! It's time to get up for school!"* — reminding you every 5 minutes that it's time to get up and start your day.

There will be no one asking you what time you will be home.

No parent pestering you to finish your homework.

Your parents will no longer be around to check on your every move.

Most young people reading this are probably thinking… *YEAH!!!!! YES!!!! ALRIGHT!!!! FINALLY!!!!* But the reality is that now what happens in your life is up to you. It's your turn to show the world what kind of person you are. It's your turn to be the grown up and, sadly, many people discover that being a grown-up is not as much fun as they thought it was going to be. This is the period of your life when you must start making decisions about your future and then take the consequences of your choices. If you were an irresponsible kid that was always able to put one over on Mom & Dad, that is no longer going to be a good option for you if you hope to become a good and respected member of the human race. However, if you make informed and mature choices, your chances of becoming a responsible and productive adult go way up.

If you are lucky enough to go directly from high school to college, these four years of higher learning will help to define who you are, thanks to the choices you make, and the choices you make will determine what kind of adult you become. This is the time when you will be revealing your character to the world and building a reputation in the form of a permanent record that will follow you throughout the rest of your life. How you perform in college, along with all the skills and knowledge you gain from this meaningful educational opportunity, will kick off your career and potentially have a big impact on your future.

As you prepare for your first semester at college, you will attend a freshman orientation for new students that will acquaint you with your new school. During this presentation, as you sit among many other students who, like you, feel excited to be accepted as a student but also nervous about being on their own for the first time, a school admissions representative will probably say something like, "Look at the student to your right and then look at the student to your left. At the end of the next four years, only one of you will graduate."

Will you be the Graduate?

Many schools use this sort of scare tactic because they want to get your attention and make you think. They want you to understand that college is more than just getting away from home so you can party. If college isn't hard work, then you won't be creating a good foundation of the basic knowledge you will need to climb your money mountain and make a good life for yourself. You need to work hard in college, and that requires discipline and time-management skills along with the motivation and desire to succeed. Your success or failure in school is yours and yours alone.

Some students opt to attend a vocational school rather than a four-year university. Vocational schools train you on specific skills and trades, offering an wide array of opportunities that can help you to begin a high paying career without attending a four-year institution. Vocational schools offer a variety of educational careers such as bookkeeping, auto mechanic, plumbing, computer programming, and many more.

While in college or vocational school, use your time to grow as a person. Make like a sponge and absorb all the information available so that you will be prepared to start your career. A great place to start is the library. Learn how to use your school's library and all the resources available in it. If you don't know enough about using the library's resources...ASK! Libraries contain more information than you will ever need to know, but finding what you need to know is sometimes tricky if you don't know your way around. Librarians can be a big help because they know the library better than anyone, and the best news of all is that they are always eager to help you find what you need. Libraries are also great quiet places to study.

And when it comes to your professors, make it your business to discover who the university's best teachers are in your chosen course of study and get to know them. These teachers will have the credentials and experience to help you expand your vision and learning. If you excel in your course work, they may offer guidance and suggestions in starting your career. They may know about internships with a prominent company, or they may recommend you to be a teacher's assistant at the college.

Your possibilities are endless if, and only if, you are able to make the best of your college learning experience. Use the services your school's career center offers to students. Get involved in the schools clubs, fraternities, or sororities. As you approach graduation, the career center's staff on campus will work to help you locate a job using all the skills and knowledge you acquired in college.

The time you spend pursuing a higher education can be a fantastic time in your life. Have fun, meet people, establish lifelong friendships with other students, but always remember that the number one reason you're in school is to learn. A good education will provide you with the tools and knowledge you will need as you climb up the money mountain. For those students that tough it out and make it all the way to graduation day, the diploma you receive at the end of your senior year will make all your work meaningful and worthwhile. And best of all, your diploma will make your future successes that much easier to achieve.

"Our goals can only be reached through a vehicle of a plan, in which we must fervently believe, and upon which we must vigorously act. There is no other route to success."

Stephen A. Brennan

Another important secret to success in business is setting goals. If you set goals and devise written plans on how to accomplish your goals, you will in time discover that you have amazingly achieved all your goals. Those who do not achieve their goals, more than likely, had no written plans. People often think that writing goals down on paper isn't really necessary. Or possibly, they simply have no idea what they want and how to get it. Or maybe they just fear failure. The bottom line is that you must set goals, write down how you plan to accomplish them, and then execute your plan. If you do this, in time you will have achieved your goals.

Just imagine if Albert Einstein, after failing an entrance exam to an engineering school in Zurich, felt he could not achieve his dreams, and simply gave up on his goals. His many accomplishments in life might never have occurred. Fortunately for all of us, a year later he repeated the entrance exam and passed. The rest is history.

What if the Wright brothers felt that their dream of flying was not possible? Would planes have ever been invented?

How about a poor, southern man named Abraham Lincoln. If he had been told that he was too tall and not handsome enough to run for political office after he lost his first election, might he have given up? Where might we as a nation be today if he had believed in the words of others instead of believing in himself and his goals?

Working hard to accomplish your goals and ambitions is worth so much. It is better to try and risk failure than to give up because you fear failing to achieve your goals.

Remember you are who you want to be and plan to be. And you can be the best.

Here are some tips on setting your goals:

1. **What do you really want?** Make sure that your goals are what you really want and write down each goal using a positive statement. Be sure not to write about what you DON'T want. Be positive.

2. **Be specific and write it down in detail.** Start with long term goals that can be achieved in three to five years,

though you may choose any length of time. Next, work on the short term goals that will make your long-term goals achievable. Work backwards and make your goals attainable. Start with each long-term goal and plan each step that will be required to get there, going from completion of your goals, to making the first call that will begin the process. Be sure to include dates, times and amounts. Being specific means be meticulously specific. Saying "I want a new home" isn't good enough. Saying "I want a five bedroom, three bath home with a gorgeous view of the Appalachian Mountains and a three car garage" is specific.

3. **Get a complete picture of where you want to go.** Map out your goals in the areas of: family and home; financial and career; spiritual and ethical; physical health; social and cultural; as well as, intellectual and educational. Maybe there are other areas of life that are important to you. Be creative.

4. **Think big.** Too many people believe that they cannot achieve their wildest dreams. Never limit your dreams. Reach higher than you think you can go. You'll be surprised how far goals can take you. But be realistic. If you look like Homer Simpson, more than likely you won't be the next George Clooney.

5. **Work the plan.** Now that you have written down, in detail, all that is required to make your dreams come true, work the plan. You may well be surprised by what happens next.

"Every job is a self portrait of the person who does it. Autograph your work with excellence."

Unknown

OK! You just got that degree from college and you're ready to conquer the world! Great! Now what?

You've got to go for it, but you've also got to be ready to work hard for long hours at a time especially in the beginning. And if you want to become a master of your profession, you must constantly work in your chosen field. Becoming an expert in your profession will be a big help in climbing up your money mountain.

Often, young people just out of college think that, because they have graduated with a new degree, they are experts in their field. The reality is that they have a lot of book knowledge but virtually no real life work experience.

Work experience gained from a thorough knowledge of your field of endeavor in the business world takes time. Your first real job after college can be both exciting and intimidating. You might feel as if you can accomplish anything and are completely unstoppable. Before your first day on the job, you may even have your sights set on your next job in the organization.

A survey of recent college graduates would probably show that most young people entering the world of business think that they are going to rise quickly up the corporate ladder of success. They expect to show their new employer just how great they are and how lucky the company is to have had the wisdom to hire them.

Even with all your certainty that everything you have worked so hard for is within reach, at some level deep down inside, you're probably just as scared as you were the day you had to go to the doctor's office for your first immunization shot. That tight feeling in the pit of your stomach is not a bad thing. It is connected to the strength you need to succeed. Most all people get a knot in their stomach when they face their own fears. Before a show most performers feel for a moment that they might not be able to go on. Their fears of failure and of not living up their own expectations grip them so strongly that they sometimes actually feel sick to their stomach.

The good news is that it is not fatal. Yes, you may well feel nervous but, if you have worked hard and are prepared, you can move forward with confidence knowing that you have all the tools required to be successful at your new job. You will, of course, need training so that you can learn the requirements of your new position. You will need to learn from your managers exactly what is expected from you as you gain knowledge and experience in the industry that employs you.

Learning all you can from your manager and other skilled employees will help you gain the knowledge and experience you will need to be a valuable contributor to the company, and to help you get to the next step up the mountain.

Always ask for help when you need it, but show your bosses that you're committed to excelling at your job and to growing within the company. Ask your manager lots of questions. A good manager knows you're new and inexperienced. Show them that you want to learn from them and do the best you can to help the organization grow. Align yourself with experienced, professional, and highly regarded co-workers.

Avoid building too close a relationship with employees that are always complaining because more than likely they will not help you to grow as an employee. Even if you view this first job as merely a stepping stone, it is never the less an excellent opportunity for you to increase your knowledge and get a great start on your chosen career path. This first job will help you get your next job. Working responsibly and showing initiative will make you more likely to get an in-company promotion.

As you progress in your job, make note of your achievements and keep track of them for your resume. Your achievements will make you more marketable when you decide to apply for a job at another company.

It is important to realize that there are always new people being educated and trained who can replace you. You are one of many at this stage of your life that can do your job. Remember you just got that fancy diploma, but are not an expert. In fact, you must be aware that in twelve months a whole new set of graduates will be ready to take your job, not to mention other employees in the company. You must always stay ahead of your competition.

No one is indispensable, but the more you learn and improve your skills, the better are your chances for career growth. As you get older, always remember that there are lots of others who can do your job. *The secret to your success is continuously working to enhance your skills and making yourself valuable to your organization.* You will have a much better chance of growing and becoming an integral part to the organization you represent, or to another company in the future, if you remember this important point. You want the company to need you, but you do not want to be in the position of needing them. Always be on the lookout for career options, but most important, you must prove to your employer that you are unique, and you offer them skills that are hard to find in other people.

"Knowledge itself is power."

Sir Francis Bacon

The World Economy & Globalization

OK. Let's say you have your first job and you're slowly, but surely, moving up the corporate ladder here in America. You believe that if you work hard, continually improve your skills, and learn all there is about your chosen profession then you can keep ahead of your competition and move ever so closer to your mountain's peak.

There is a lot of truth in your belief that you have the potential to succeed, but there is more to the story. You are competing with the best and brightest America has to offer, but you are also competing with the best and the brightest people from all around the world. Knowing your American competition is important, but you had better also know how the rest of the world can affect your job and your future employment. The world today is much different than the one your parents grew up in. Today, thousands of multinational firms operate businesses in countries all around the world. A multinational firm is a company that has manufacturing facilities in at least one country other than their home country. They operate their business from a global perspective. There are no longer easily-defined borders and markets to compete in, as the world is now the marketplace.

The world today has become a mass merchandise mart, where trade occurs 24 hours a day, 7 days a week, and only strong and innovative companies will survive in the future. The growth of multinational firms has helped fuel the economic growth in many of the world's developing countries. For instance, many products used in the United States are manufactured by U.S. firms in other countries where wages and the cost of manufacturing are less. After the manufacturing process is completed, the finished product is shipped back to America for the U.S. consumer to purchase.

With Globalization, many of these countries are now manufacturing their own competitive products to ship directly to the U.S. consumer. When other countries cheaply manufacture products similar to those being produced by U.S. companies, world competition increases and more pressure is put on the U.S. manufacturer to create a better product, to stay ahead of competitors around the world.

Take a look at the economic growth of China. President Nixon, in an issue of Foreign Affairs Magazine, cautioned that continuing to ignore China was both unrealistic and unwise: "We simply cannot afford to leave China forever outside the family of nations, there to nurture its fantasies, cherish its hates, and threaten its neighbors." In 1972, President Nixon was the first President to ever travel to China, and it was assumed his visit would open the economic door to this vast nation. However, because of President Nixon's involvement in the Watergate Scandal and his eventual resignation from office, the United States did not open full diplomatic relations with China until 1979. From 1979 to 2005, it is estimated that China's Gross Domestic Product grew at an annual rate of 9.6%, according to a Congressional Research Report.

In 2006, China's economy grew at 11.1% and it is now estimated that China's total annual economic output is $2.7 trillion in U.S. Currency, as reported by the National Bureau of Statistics. It should soon pass the third largest economy in the world, Germany with an estimated economy of $3 trillion and Japan with an annual economic output of $4.2 trillion. Many economists expect that, if China continues to implement economic reforms on its people and businesses, it will in the coming years become the biggest economy in the world, surpassing the United States' current $12.9 trillion Gross Domestic Product.

China, with its rapidly growing exports of goods to the United States, is putting increasing pressure on U.S. business interests, both domestically and in foreign markets, to adapt to the ever changing world financial markets.

As of early 2007, China holds $1.2 trillion in Foreign Cash Reserves, and its reserves are growing at $1.5 billion a day.

Foreign Cash Reserves are made up primarily of 60% U.S. dollars, 30% Euros (currency of European nations), and the remainder in British Pounds and Japanese Yen. China is now the second biggest owner of U.S. Treasury securities behind Japan. Some say that this increasing ownership of U.S. Treasury Securities may give some leverage to China's economic influence with the United States in the future. For example, if the Chinese government stopped buying U.S. Treasuries, the Dollar would plunge in value and the United States Federal Reserve Board would have to increase interest rates to stabilize the currency.

China is also trying to purchase international companies to expand its reach on the global economic stage and to gain more recognition in the world. Chinese investments in U.S. companies included the purchase of IBM's Personal Computer Division by the Chinese company Lenovo for $1.2 billion in 2004. China's economic growth, along with its position on the world stage as host country to the 2008 Olympics in Beijing, has put this vast country out front for the world to see.

China is not without its problems. Concerns, over recalls of some products manufactured in China and shipped to the U.S., have alarmed some politicians in regard to the Chinese Government's ability to inspect the products it exports. In addition, China's central bank will need to slow down the country's growth to prevent inflation from rising too quickly. Too high an increase in growth could result in an increase in prices that would be too much for the country's poor to afford. Even though China is experiencing unparalleled growth in its economy, the wealth has not found its way to many of the country's people. This is why China must slow down its growth, or risk inflation.

In the coming years, as the Chinese standard of living improves, there is much concern about the amount of the world's resources that China's 1.2 billion people will consume. The entire world population will undoubtedly see a tremendous growing competition with China for our planet's resources of oil, steel, concrete, automobile products, and so much more.

Another country that continues to expand its economic base and compete on the world stage is India. The world's largest democracy of over 1 billion people has improved its manufacturing sector, building a better business infrastructure with improved worker productivity. Some economists believe that India's economic expansion could experience double digit growth over the next few years. With tremendous investment from foreign companies located in the United States, Japan , as well as those in Europe, the Chinese and Indian economies are driving demand for new housing, improved roads, and bridges.

India has become the place for many U.S. and Multinational firms to outsource many of their services, such as call centers and back office operations. The companies find that the cost savings are substantial and, since India's population mostly speaks English and produces an annual output of 2.5 million new graduates each year, finding cheap skilled workers is easy. However, with Indian graduates skilled in engineering, for example, coming to the marketplace each year looking for work and being paid a third of what a U.S. worker is compensated, the potential is for more U.S. outsourcing of services, spreading far beyond call services and back office operations.

India is doing well today economically as compared to its past, yet 260,000 million of its citizens still live in poverty, earning less than $1.00 a day. This is why India must control its growth or risk inflation, which could result in many of the country's poor having difficulty purchasing goods such as food. As India's government invests in its infrastructure and improves conditions like clean water and sanitation, the economic impact will be felt all across India, and might even help them to surpass China's rate of growth in the future.

China and India are but two examples of countries in the world that are slowly growing in wealth, and in time, as they improve their technologies, education, sanitation, and living standards for the majority of their people, their economic power will grow in the world.

Today, globalization of the world's markets is open to so many countries and, as world trade is almost borderless, you will find an ever-changing and dynamic business world. Multinational Corporations, with a need for critically-skilled employees, will recruit the best skilled from across the world to find just the right people to make their corporations grow on the world stage.

It is important, as you climb your money mountain, that you understand world economies and international commerce, and how it can affect your job in the future. You must constantly learn, and build on your skills, to ensure that your position does not ever become outsourced to another firm or country.

Business organizations are in the business of making money, and you must show them that you are a critical asset to their organization. Globalization and multinational firms are here to stay, and each country is going to do its best to build top-notch organizations with products and services that are in demand by other countries of the world and their citizens.

Be prepared.

Ethics

Chapter 9

"I consider ethics to be an exclusively human concern without any super human authority behind it."

Albert Einstein

Ethics and Professionalism

Two of the most important words used in the course of human events in the modern world are Ethics and Professionalism. These are powerful words that most people say they incorporate into their daily lives. However, when their actions are exposed to the sunshine that comes with public scrutiny, it too often becomes clear that indeed they live a life lacking in both ethical behavior and professionalism.

From business and governmental leaders to professional athletes, you will often hear people assert that many around them are unethical; however, they insist that they personally live up to the highest ethical and professional standards. Though, their behavior may eventually prove them wrong. Business leaders, like those who headed up the once powerful multibillion dollar energy firm Enron, repeatedly assert their high ethical and professional standards. Yet it was illegal and unethical actions of the executives at Enron that resulted in their company's downfall, costing thousands of employees a secure future, when they lost their retirement accounts and pensions. These former Enron executives are just a few of the many who have forgotten the importance of ethics and professionalism, if they actually ever comprehended the meaning of the words.

Throughout the history of America, there has been no end to the list of government leaders who put their own interests ahead of their constituents, only to find themselves brought in front of an Ethics Committee or a court of law. Each one of these betrayers of the public's trust ignored the importance of ethical and professional behavior.

It is important that you always stay on the right path in both your personal and professional life. Nothing is worth tarnishing your reputation or your integrity as you ascend up to your mountain's peak.

A person with integrity is one who steadfastly adheres to a strict moral or ethical code, instead of just talking about it. Simply said, *integrity is doing the right thing for the common good even when no one is looking.*

Do not allow yourself to ever do something that you know — *both in your heart and in your head* — is not right. Do not succumb to temptation and do something that is against your personal or professional principles.

Don't look for the easy way out, because in the end you will not find it, as it does not exist.

Every good outcome takes work. Good school grades, excellent employment reviews, smart financial planning that bring investment results, maintaining a high credit rating, developing and implementing a personal budget that is workable, all take work. A truly successful person knows that personal and professional relationships are only a few of the important things in life that require hard work to achieve positive long-lasting results.

Your focus should always be on doing the right thing because this outlook will help you to build character and a reputation as a good person. Trust your gut instincts — *that unsettling feeling in your stomach that tells you something is not right* — as a guide to help you choose the right path when you are confronted with a situation that is uncertain or uncomfortable. That unpleasant gut-wrenching feeling is there to help you to make the right decision.

You probably remember a time in school when you were taking a test and sitting next to the smartest kid in the class. You might have thought, even for a millisecond, about taking a quick look at his/her test answers, because you had a clear view and the teacher wasn't looking your way. Hopefully, you knew that would be wrong, because your head and maybe that uneasiness in your gut were telling you so. A person of integrity would make the right decision and let their test grade be a result of their hard work and ability, instead of a result of their classmate's hard work and ability. You will feel better about yourself in the long run if you make the right decision to be honest.

Think back when you were very young. Perhaps you were in line with your mom at the grocery store when you spotted your favorite candy on the shelf near the checkout stand. You begin to bug your mom that you WANT a piece of candy, and you WANT it now. Your mom says it is too close to dinner now, but maybe next time. You begin to freak out as if you are possessed. Your mom looks around, hoping that no one is watching your breakdown, but when she sees that everyone is watching, she is immediately angry, thanks to this ridiculous scene. When your mother finishes paying the cashier and you both leave the store, your mother is probably thinking about your upcoming punishment. All she wants to do is get out of that parking lot and get you home. And you, in five minutes time, completely forget about the candy ordeal, only to be reminded of it by your mother on the drive home.

Hopefully, as you got older, you matured and got past those moments of alien-like behavior, right up until the time you became a teenager and your hormones went berserk. During these years, there is a very real possibility that your parents felt as if they were witnessing Linda Blair's character in a movie from their generation, The Exorcist. That character was so possessed by demons that she required an exorcism. Or perhaps you were a little more like the pod people in the movie Invasion of the Body Snatchers. Either way, your parents knew that those moments of insanity were temporary, and that their real child would return sooner or later.

No matter how you acted out, even at those most severe moments of lunacy, you knew deep down that your behavior was wrong. Hopefully, you have learned that there are unpleasant consequences that come your way as a result of wrong behavior. Perhaps you had to miss some of your favorite activities for a while because you were grounded for a few days.

If you haven't learned about Newton's Law of reciprocal actions, it's time you did. For every action, there is an equal but opposite reaction, which means that when you do something wrong, the universe will push back and something negative will come your way. *What goes around comes around,* some people say. So be careful of your actions and consider the consequences, because you will have to live with the consequences of your actions. The rest of society is not nearly as forgiving as parents can be.

Most professions today, along with their business and professional associations, issue standards of ethical behavior and professionalism to which all their employees or members must adhere, or risk termination from the company, or expulsion from the group. As you climb higher and higher up the path of your mountain, never compromise your integrity and always live by the ethical and professional standards that you know are correct. If you do this, you will stay on the right path in life. Your personal and business ethics and professionalism are essential for you to grow, and ultimately reach the peak of your mountain.

*"Bad officials are elected by good citizens
who do not vote."*

George Jean Nathan

Your Vote Counts

As I am writing this chapter, I am watching the election re-
turns for Election '06. The result of the election is not what is
most important to me. What is most important to me, is the
American electoral process that stems from our constitutional
right to vote. Ever since I turned 18, I have made it a point to
gather and assess the information I need to know about the
issues affecting me, so that on Election Day, I can make an
informed decision about my vote. Each election year, I think
about the men and woman who have protected and defended

my right to vote. I know that the freedom I have in my life today is a result of sacrifices made by those who came before us, and sacrifices that many continue to make today. Some of these great men and women made the ultimate sacrifice of their lives in an effort to defend our national way of life.

I often wonder what might these heroes who sacrificed their life for our country have accomplished in their lifetime, had they lived?

Perhaps one of them would have become a future president, or a renowned doctor who could have cured cancer; maybe a Grammy-winning musician, or a teacher who could have opened the eyes and minds of a generation of young people. We will never know, but one thing is certain: they gave their lives to protect the land they believed to be the greatest country in the world, where the only person who can stop you from achieving your goals and aspirations is you. NO ONE has the right to tell you that, because of your upbringing, your religious affiliation, or the color of your skin, you cannot do something great. The only one, that can prevent you from achieving your dreams, is you.

Many Americans today feel that their vote does not count, and you may be among them. Many believe that politics is crooked and often politicians think only of themselves, their special interest friends, personal power and remaining in power. Unfortunately, sometimes this is true, but we must hold onto the hope that most politicians, on both sides of the aisle, ultimately want what is best for the country and their constituents. If, however, we see that a politician puts self-interest first and special interests second, then we, the people of the United States of America, need to assert our interests and hold our elected officials' feet to the proverbial fire of a red hot electorate on Election Day.

But to be able to hold an elected official accountable for bad behavior, you've got to know the difference between right and wrong in American government.

You need to pay attention so you can know who the players are. You need to understand the rules of the game so you can recognize an infraction when you see one. If only the American people would look at American politics with the same interest they take in reality television shows, like *Survivor Island*, life would be better in America. It is a mystery to me why Americans aren't particularly interested in the shenanigans that take place in our government every day. It is just as interesting as any reality television show, and often more interesting than American sports. You've got mavericks, honorable coalitions, and committee intrigue among the heroes and villains who walk the halls of our state and national capitols every day.

C-SPAN is a great place to start learning about politics and politicians, because it is unfiltered by the "news media". You get to hear what a politician actually says before a "news personality" puts his or her personal spin on what they heard the politician say. You might be surprised to learn that what you hear is completely different from what the "news personality" says they heard. If C-SPAN moves too slowly for you, you can catch politicians of all political stripes engaging in sharp-tongued verbal combat on cable TV almost every night. Give it a try. You might like it even more than the *Survivor Island* intrigue. Capitol Hill intrigue affects your life more directly than Reality Television ever could.

While you are young, your views of the world may be very different than when you are older. Some say, that as you get older, you become a little more tolerant and conservative than when you are young. Some say just the opposite. I have no idea which is true. What I do know for a fact is that one vote can make a difference.

Think about the 2000 Presidential election. Then Governor of Texas, George W. Bush won the Presidency of the United States from Vice President Al Gore by only 537 votes. The outcome of the November 2000 presidential election was delayed, while Florida tried to verify a correct vote count. After the election was certified by Florida Secretary of State Katharine Harris, the Supreme Court of Florida overturned that certification, saying Florida law demanded that all ballots be counted if the voter's intention could be determined. Then on December 12, 2000, the United States Supreme Court in a 5 to 4 decision, issued its ruling in *Bush v. Gore*. The majority in the court said that the ballot recount, then being conducted in certain counties in the State of Florida, must be stopped, due to the lack of a consistent standard of recount methods from county to county. It was then that Governor Bush was deemed the winner of the presidential election. After millions of votes were cast all across the nation, the election was decided by a razor-thin margin of only 537 votes in Florida. If Al Gore had received just one vote more in 538 of Florida's 5,885 voting precincts, he would have received Florida's Electoral Votes, and he would have been sworn in as the President of the United States of America.

It is important in each election year that you learn about the candidates and the proposed legislation that will have a big effect on your life, on both a local and national level.

In a few years, your generation will transition into your roles as the current leaders of our country. Perhaps you will be one of those leaders. It is your responsibility to ensure that you, and your future children, cast a vote on Election Day, because that is the one day out of 365 in a year when your voice will be heard. Voting is one of the most unique expressions of democracy, and one that should never be taken for granted.

Vote with pride and always remember that knowledge is power, especially in a voting booth.

Identity Theft

Chapter

"Every seventy nine seconds a thief steals someone identity."

CBS News

Let's look into the future and say that you've done everything right. You moved in the right direction up your money mountain, all the while getting closer to reaching your mountain's peak. You chose to stay in school, building on the knowledge that helped you secure your first career position.

You started to make a little money, and positioned yourself so that you could not only make more money, but could become the best that you could be, both in your life and in your career.

The mountain climb to this point was hard but not impossible, as you painstakingly maneuvered through school, learned about credit, set up bank accounts, interviewed and accepted your first job. You can almost see the peak of the mountain, and in time, if all continues to go as you planned, you will conquer your mountain's crest, and undoubtedly celebrate your achievements with joy and accolades from yourself and others.

It is such a promising scenario, full of hope with absolutely no downside. Unfortunately, life is known to throw you a curve ball every now and then, and even if you are looking out for those unexpected twists and turns, you can still find yourself in a mess. Though there are many unavoidable obstacles in life, there is one disastrous complication that you need to avoid, if you can, because it can cause the rocks on your mountain's slope to loosen, and bring you tumbling down.

This very dangerous and unforgiving obstacle is called Identity Theft. Identity Theft is a crime that occurs when someone steals your name and other personal information, to commit fraud. If you are a victim of identity theft, your superior credit score, that you worked so hard to build, could easily be ruined before you even know what's happening.

According to Equifax, criminals steal a person's identity to open new credit cards accounts, buy vehicles, counterfeit check and debit cards, and they may even take all the money you have in your bank accounts. These are just some of the crimes Identity Thieves commit while pretending to be you. They could sell your personal information to other criminals, who will then use your identity for illegal immigration purposes, or they may simply use your identity to get a cell phone account that will be used for criminal activity. Think that this can't happen to you...*THINK AGAIN. It can and it will unless you protect yourself against it.*

Let's look at the facts:

- According to the New York Times, 27 million Americans have been victims of identity theft in just the last 5 years.

- In one year, Knight Ridder/Tribune Business News estimates that 500,000 Americans will be robbed of their identities, with more than $4 billion stolen in their names.

- Every 79 seconds, a thief steals someone's identity, opens accounts in the victim's name, and goes on a buying spree says CBSnews.com.

- CNNFN.com says experts have found, it takes a victim from 6 months to two years to recover from Identity Theft. That is 6 months to two years of hard, frustrating work just to get back to where you started.

We all would like to believe that bad things won't happen to us, but this is a crime that may very well happen to you, if you don't watch your step. So, if you want to ascend to the peak of your mountain, do your very best to avoid becoming a victim of identity theft. Here are some of the ways that a thief steals your identity according to Equifax:

- Criminals go through your trash, looking for bank or credit statements or some other form of identification, like tax records, receipts, etc.

- They may steal your wallet so they can acquire your credit cards, driver's license and bank cards. Once they have something with your name on it, they can go to the post office and file a change of address form in your name, so that all your mail then comes directly to them.

- Acquiring your personal records at work.

- Obtaining your credit reports, by posing as your land-lord who has a lawful right to the information.

- Acquiring personal information you share on un-secured sites on the Internet.

- Buying personal information about you from an inside source, such as an employee at a department or retail store where you shop.

Do not be fooled, Identity Theft is the fastest growing white collar crime in America. Banks, credit card companies and Internet web sites are constantly changing their security and encryption data to reduce the chance of you becoming a victim. Let's look at some ways you can become a victim of this crime, without even realizing that your actions are offering up your personal information.

Let's say that you have a **MySpace.com** or **Facebook.com** account. You describe yourself in detail — where you went to school, where you live, your hobbies, your pets, your favorite music, where you work, etc. Just think about the information you are putting out there for the world to see. Identity thieves now have access to lots of personal information about you, and they have a picture of you. They may even be able to find more information about you, by doing random searches on the internet.

Now think about all the websites you visit, and the passwords you choose to access your sites. Are your User ID's and pass-words similar to information that may be easily discovered in public chat rooms, on **MySpace.com**, and related sites? For example, do you use simple user ID's like your first name, and a password like a pet's name, or a birthday? It may be easy for someone to figure out your user ID's and passwords. Always be sure that your User ID's and passwords have absolutely no connection to anything about you that is public knowledge.

Another growing scam is receiving e-mail that appears to be coming from a reliable source. It is called *Phishing*. The e-mail may look exactly like your bank or credit card company's main web page, but in reality, it is just some scam artist looking for you to give up personal information.

Think you are too smart to be caught in this phishing expedition? Don't fool yourself. There are countless smart, capable people, just like you, who thought they were too smart to be fooled, who are now living with the consequences. If these scam artists were unsuccessful at preying on the innocent, they would find another line of work. Instead, they are working hard each and every day to find a way to your personal information. So be prepared.

If you need to do online business with your bank or any financial institution, where you are required to give personal and private information, always go to that website on your own initiative by turning on your Web Browser and typing in the web address. **NEVER** click on a link in an e-mail that takes you to a page where you are required to type in personal information, like User ID's and passwords.

Here's another creative tool that the bad guys like to use. They call you at home and tell you they are calling from your bank or credit card provider's security office. Or, sometimes they are offering you a winning prize, like a free cruise and just need to confirm your birth date and Social Security Number. They insist that they must confirm this information. **NEVER** give them the information. Get their telephone number and name, and tell them you will call back. You likely will hear a click on the line, indicating they hung up. If they give you a number, do not call that number. Look up the phone number of the company in question, like your bank or credit card company, and call the company directly, to confirm the call was indeed from their company.

There are many ways scam artists can trick you, and even the brightest of people can be fooled. Con artists are good at what they do. They are professional liars and you can easily become their victim. So, always be on guard, and odds are you will save yourself from becoming a victim of identity theft.

Where should you store your many access ID's and passwords? Are they stored on a notebook computer, which can be stolen? How about in your purse or wallet? *Not a good idea.* If you must right them down, store them in a place that has no connection to computers, and don't actually write the exact passwords. Write down a reminder, that only you will understand.

The chances of you being a victim of Identity Theft, through an online account where you pay bills or access your banking information, is small, because these firms spend millions of dollars protecting their clients' information. However, you must be aware of just how easy it is for someone to get your personal information, from the most innocent of things you do each and every day.

Do you throw out your bills, receipts, bank statements, and other personal information without first shredding them? **DON'T!!** *Always shred your personal papers before throwing them in the trash.*

Do you look closely around you when you withdraw money from an ATM? Is someone looking over your shoulder as you are in putting your password into the ATM? Could someone be watching too closely?

Do you leave personal information in your car's glove box? You must always have your insurance card and registration in the car, but is there another place to keep it, that is not as obvious as the glove box. What about the purchase agreement for your car? It may also be in the glove box, and it has all the information an ID thief could ever need.

If you want to continue your climb up your money mountain, without stumbling back, then you must protect your personal information. Becoming a victim of Identity Theft will not only cost a lot of money, it will also be one of the most stressful events in your life, and it will make that climb back up your mountain much harder.

"The most important trip you may take in life is meeting people half way."

Henry Boyle

As you work hard to climb your money mountain, you will need to save and invest a portion of your income, so that years from now, when your retirement comes, you will have more choices on how to spend the latter years of your life.

In your life, there are some things that are simply non-negotiable, but a lot more than you may think is negotiable. Your negotiating skills will determine how many of your hard earned dollars are left for you to save.

You will also find much of your current monthly income spent on necessities, like food, clothes, and a place to live. So each month, a big chunk of your money will go to pay for the essentials, like your rent, electric, telephone, food, and maybe even cable television, if you consider that an essential.

Then we come to what is left over, after you pay the essentials. Many call it your disposable income. You will find a world of retailers, working hard to convince you to spend your extra money on life's expensive toys, like high-priced cars, gorgeous furniture, hi-speed computers, and big screen televisions. The temptation that an effective advertising and marketing campaign can have on a consumer is powerful. And the people who want your money don't care if you are spending extra cash or your life savings. They just want the sale, so don't spend your future on high priced products that you do not need. Too many people don't realize that there is a very big difference between need and want. Marketing plays on your desires, your wants and your ego while leaving your financial security completely out of the equation.

Today's market place is filled with so many great and exciting new products. You will naturally succumb to your desire to occasionally purchase some of these items. You just have to have a plan, know your limits, and learn to get the best bargain for your dollar.

Each holiday season, the electronic and print media go on and on about the latest hot holiday gifts that are all the rage. Consumers, who are driven by their desires, become so desperate to possess this fabulous new product immediately, that they will spend much more than the retail value of the product, just so they can buy it first. One item during Christmas 2006, that was a "must have", was the Sony Play Station 3. This computer game player was in such high demand during the holidays that many people camped out at department store entrances across the United States for three days, just so they could be first to buy one of these $600 play stations. Others purchased the same product on eBay for as much as $3,000, spending up to five times its value, just so they could possess the newest hot ticket gadget. If they had just waited a few extra weeks, they could have found the product in the stores for the regular price. And maybe, if they had shopped smart, they could have bought it at a discounted price.

Most young people, as they are graduating from high school and college, dream about what their life will be like. Most hope that they can retire young, and be very wealthy. We often see entertainers, athletes, and successful business people, who possess the very best the world's marketplace has to offer. Their incredible wealth has given them the freedom to buy without even thinking about the cost. Sure, they may have lots of money now, but that lucrative career can come to an unexpected screeching halt for so many reasons, and when that happens, they will probably wish they had been more careful about how they spent their money when they had lots of it.

When a person has lots of money from a large income, with lots more to come, the idea of asking for a better price, or waiting for the product to go on sale may never even enter their mind. They want it, and they want it now! They want the ego gratification, and the sheer pleasure of buying it at that instant, rather than waiting for a sale, or asking the merchant for a better price. We have all heard stories about people who made it big early in life, and then spent their money carelessly with little regard to savings for their old age, only to realize too late, that there will be no retirement and they will have to work until they die. Not a happy realization.

Just as it is important for you to work hard, it is equally important for you to think before you recklessly spend money you have worked so hard to earn. Staying on top of your money mountain will take work. How you spend your money, during the years you are building your wealth, will determine how much money you have when the time comes for you to kick back, take it easy, and enjoy the latter years of your life. If you don't have savings, you won't be kicking back. You will be working until you are no longer physically capable of working

If you are lucky, though, you will be able to work hard to earn a good living, and then retire, while you are young enough to enjoy the freedom. If you are smart, you will learn to balance your income with your savings, and you will set goals. Too few people spend a lot of time thinking about their long term goals.

When you are young, retirement and old age seem so far away. Too many people, unfortunately, reach a time in their lives when they look back and wonder: *"What happened to all that money I earned?"* and *"How did it slip through my fingers?"* Since we will all, at times, spend our money on the things that we desire, rather than the things that we need, let's focus on a technique that can help you to buy what you desire, while saving money on the purchase.

The first thing to know is that almost everything you purchase is **negotiable**. It will be entirely up to you whether the money you earn is spent responsibly or wasted. Learning how to negotiate will help you to spend your money more responsibly.

When two parties agree on a price for a service or product, and the transaction is a win-win outcome for both parties, it's called a negotiated settlement. When most people think "business negotiations", they think "corporate board rooms", but negotiations can take place in any business deal. Negotiations can take place in a purchase you make for either personal or business use, for things like food and clothing, or the interest rate you receive on your invested savings, as well as the interest rate you pay on your car loan.

A capitalist society is supposed to breed competition among businesses, to price products and services so that we, as consumers, will want to buy them. You, as a buyer of goods and services, should try to get what you believe is a fair price when you spend your money.

In today's marketplace, you are not limited to your local retailer when you wish to buy a new television, for example, simply because that retailer is located near your home. The Internet can be a valuable tool to help you compare the selling price of products that many companies are selling all across the nation.

Let's say, for example, a new Plasma Television sells at a local retailer near your home for $2,599. You then go to another local retailer, and see that they are selling that exact same TV for $2,499. When you search the Internet, you find an online retailer selling that same television on their website, with home delivery included in the price, for only $2,399. You may even be able to avoid paying state sales tax by purchasing the item from an online retailer.

When the online retailer has the best price, print a copy of the product page with the online price, then go to the manager of your local retailer, and ask if they are willing to match the price. If they are willing to match the price, you can save money and the local retailer can make a sale.

The worst the local retailer can say is "No". Or, they might make a counteroffer. They may try to persuade you that paying the higher price is smart because of their local customer service and quick delivery, when you purchase from them locally. This may be a consideration for you, and it may not. Remember, that when you order on the Internet, some large national retailers will allow you to pick up the TV, at a store near you, rather than waiting for it to be shipped. In any case, you can always save money by just asking for a better price. Most likely, the local retailer will make an offer to lower his price to secure the sale, possibly at a price slightly higher than the Internet merchant. They may also provide free home delivery.

Always be polite to the salesperson and store manager, and they will try to help you, if they can, because they want the sale.

Is the money you can save worth a few minutes of research? That is for you to decide, but in this example, you may have saved as much as $200 on the television and received free delivery. If you do your research, and negotiate with retailers, you may even be able to build a long term business relationship with that retailer. So, what might you do with the $200 you were able to save on your purchase? Maybe buy food, clothing, or perhaps invest your savings so you can earn more money.

Remember, you are always looking for a win-win situation, and if you don't ask for a better price, you may be paying more than you should.

So, let's look at what it takes to negotiate in order to save money on the items you plan to purchase.

First, know what you want, and what the product sells for at Internet sites and local merchants near your home.

Second, do not be nervous about asking for a better price, and do not be afraid to walk away from a merchant. if you're not happy with the price they're giving you.

In a later chapter you will read about buying a car. This is one negotiation that can save you thousands, if you spend a little time researching the vehicle before you buy. Another big purchase, where you can save a lot of cash, is buying a home. Only time will tell if the purchase of your first home will turn out to be a great investment, or a bad deal. The outcome will be based, to a large extent, on research and negotiations that take place right up to the time you finalize that purchase.

Negotiating is not rocket science. You, simply, are asking a seller to match, or beat, another seller's price. If you learn to negotiate in a professional and polite manner, you will find that over the years you can save thousands of dollars.

*"Never spend your money before
you have it."*

Thomas Jefferson

You are beginning to earn an income and, as you ascend
up your mountain, it is going to be very important for your
financial future, that you spend the money you earn wisely.
You may detect a theme developing. That is because it cannot
be stressed often enough that informed spending is wiser
spending.

Whether you make hundreds of dollars a month or many
thousands of dollars a month, creating and maintaining a financial budget is important to your success.

A budget helps you plan for today, and build a financial nest egg for tomorrow. The best way, to formulate and then carry out a sound financial plan, is to draft a budget that will clearly display on paper, exactly how you spend your money.

If you are like most people, your eyes are currently rolling back in your head, at the very sight of the word "budget". *Oh, no! NOT a budget!* It is understandable. "Budget" is, to some, a four letter word. Hopefully, though, as budgeting is discussed in this chapter, you will begin to see, that a budget can be a very advantageous tool in helping you to chart exactly where your money is spent each month. Seeing how you spend your money on paper, or a computer screen, gives you a real picture of your cash flow, so that you can visualize clearly where your money is going, and how it is working for you.

Once you have analyzed your cash flow and have a complete understanding of your overall financial picture, you should be able to see that "budget" does not have to be a scary word. A budget is a rewarding asset that can help you to be creative and flexible with your spending.

In the banking chapter, we discussed opening and maintaining your own checking account. To budget successfully, you must know exactly where all your money goes. Creating a budget takes time and dedication, if it is to be developed and managed properly. Today's consumers use their credit and debit cards, so often, that some people haphazardly spend money, without true regard for their overall financial situation.

It is very important that you keep up to date financial information. Every time you earn income, and deposit that income into your account; use a debit card to purchase an item; or write a check to pay a bill, you must input that information into your checkbook, so you will know exactly how much money you have in your checking account, at any given time. This will prevent you from overdrawing your checking account, and make creating a budget much easier. A good way to easily confirm your withdrawals and balance your checkbook is to access your checking account online, through your bank's website.

Keeping a budget worksheet, like the one at the end of this chapter, will be a huge asset in developing, implementing and maintaining a financial plan that works.

Let's take a look at an example of how a budget can help. Let's say you earn an income of $4,000 a month, but you spend $4,200 a month. It should be obvious, that a typical spending pattern like this will not leave you with enough money to pay your bills. Keep that spending rate up, and it won't be long before you are deep in debt. The first step, in setting up a realistic workable budget, is to set up categories for your anticipated monthly Income and Expenses.

Begin your budget planning by making a list of your monthly expenses. Include all your necessities, like food, housing, insurance, transportation, electric, telephone, and possibly, Internet and television cable access. Divide these monthly expenditures up into categories on a personal budget worksheet similar to the one in Figure 1.

It will take you a few months, to really become familiar with your expenses, so that you can easily identify how much of your income you are spending on variable expense items, such as entertainment, clothes, books, dining out, and even gas for your car. Even the cash you spend on lattés, write it down.

During the first two or three months of working on your budget, keep all your receipts... yes, even the fast food restaurant and convenience store receipts. This will help you track where all your money is really going each month, and it will help you formulate a more realistic budget.

Keeping all these receipts, and itemizing your spending on paper — *or accounting software on your computer* — will help you to fine tune your expenditures each month. It will help you to uncover areas, where you spent more money than you intended, and areas where you spent less than expected. You may even identify categories during this period, which you completely left out of your plan. It will also help you to see, why you need savings for a rainy day. Unanticipated expenses occur. This month, you may need new tires for your car. Next month, it's a cellular phone that is lost or broken. It could be an unexpected doctor's visit, or maybe just a special night out, when you spent a little more than your budget, and your wallet, allowed. Saving for unexpected expenses is a far better idea, than just putting it on your credit card, and hoping for the best.

To develop a budget, you must first identify where you currently spend your money, and how much you spend. Once you see where your money goes, you can identify areas where you can improve your financial balance with spending cut backs so that you can stay on the right path, and move higher up the mountain. A budget is like a map. Follow the map, and reach your destination in the least amount of time, while creating wealth and prosperity for yourself; or, make a wrong turn by foolish overspending, and fall into debt and financial problems, that will in turn create a hazardous trail, making it difficult for you to find your path back to financial security.

There are no silver bullets that can protect you from poor financial planning. It is you who must plan how much to spend, and how much to save. Good planning will help you achieve your goals in life, and will help you to reach your mountain's peak.

Remember, a budget is a starting point, and must be somewhat flexible. Do not look at it as a chore. Look at it as a simple guide that can help you make more money, which will lead to a better and more secure financial future. You should use a budget during your climb up the mountain, because it will make it easier for you to see your assets and your liabilities, more clearly. A budget can help you to save for your first home, that new car, a wonderful vacation, or a secure retirement. If you stay on the trail of your budget map, you can get closer to your destination faster, and easier than you expected. However, if you make a wrong turn and find yourself off the path, you may discover that in today's marketplace, it will take longer, and be a more treacherous trip up your Money Mountain. Those who do no planning may not ever find a way back, and financial security could be lost to them forever.

Personal Budget

SUMMARY	ACTUAL	BUDGETED	OVER/UNDER BY	NOTES
Total Income				
Total Expenses				
Income LESS Expenses				

INCOME

DETAILS	ACTUAL	BUDGETED	OVER/UNDER BY	NOTES
Salary1				
Salary 2				
Investment				
Stocks and Bonds				
Other				
Total Income				

EXPENSES

WITHHOLDINGS	ACTUAL	BUDGETED	OVER/UNDER BY	NOTES
Federal Income Tax				
State Income Tax				
FICA				
Medical				
Other				
Total Withholdings				
Percent of Expenses				

FINANCE PAYMENTS	ACTUAL	BUDGETED	OVER/UNDER BY	NOTES
Credit Card 1				
Credit Card 2				
Student Loan				
Auto Loan				
Home Mortgage				
Personal Loan				
Total Finance Payments				
Percent of Expenses				

FIXED EXPENSES	ACTUAL	BUDGETED	OVER/UNDER BY	NOTES
Property Taxes				
Rent				
Charitable Donations				
Home Insurance				
Auto Insurance				
Life Insurance				
Medical Insurance				
Cable TV				
Telephone				
Utilities				
Total Fixed Expenses				
Percent of Expenses				

VARIABLE EXPENSES	ACTUAL	BUDGETED	OVER/UNDER BY	NOTES
Household				
Groceries				
Auto Upkeep and Gas				
Other Travel Expenses				
Furniture				
Clothing				
School				
Medical / Prescriptions				
Entertainment				
Memberships				
Dining Out				
Gifts				
Vacation				
Pet Care				
Other				
Total Variable Expenses				
Percent of Expenses				

"Remember that time is money."

Benjamin Franklin

Savings & Smart Investing

We already know that, first, you must pay for the essentials of life, like rent or mortgage payments, utilities and groceries. Then you need money for extras like clothing, cable, phone and other everyday necessities. Next, you want a little "mad money", so you can enjoy a few of life's luxuries, and have a little fun; but, before all the money is spent, you better save a little for that moment in life when you will want to quit working, and enjoy life while you still can.

You don't want to wake up one day, when you are middle-aged, and suddenly realize you didn't save any of the money you earned over the years. If this happens, you have fewer years to save for retirement, and may very well find that you have to work for the rest of your life. You want to plan, so you are in the driver's seat when the decision about retirement comes. Do not leave it up to poor planning, to make the decision for you.

You may enjoy going out on the town with friends, seeing great movies, eating in fine restaurants, and attending concerts, or professional sporting events. You may enjoy taking trips, and buying those great toys, that you don't really need. It is great fun, while it lasts, but you've got to remember, all these fun things you enjoy so much, cost money, and that's OK now, because you've got a job. Imagine, though, what it will be like when you are older and you decide to quit working.

The thought of retiring, and not having to work at least five days a week, sounds pretty good, until you start thinking about paying your bills. The bills won't stop coming in, just because you've retired. You will need money in your old age, just as much as you need it today. So, you need to think now, about how much money you will need to enjoy the good life, when you are no longer able, or willing to work. *Ideally, the amount of money you accumulate during your working life, should sustain your current standard of living, for the rest of your life after retirement.*

Believe me when I tell you that you do not want to be 65 years old with no retirement options.

There has been over the years much debate in Congress about Social Security, and how to protect it for retirees in the future. There are no guarantees that Social Security, as we know it today, will be around when you are ready to retire.

There are no guarantees that you will have a pension from an employer, just as there are no guarantees that, if you purchase a lottery ticket, you will be a winner. You must take responsibility for planning for your own future and financial well-being.

When you are ready to retire, if Social Security is in force as it is today, and if you are working for a firm that has a viable pension plan, then you may well have a financially secure retirement. Just remember, though, that nothing is certain. Remember the employees of ENRON? They thought they had planned so well for their retirement by investing in the wonderful company that employed them. They thought that, right up to the day they discovered their retirement savings were all gone, thanks to corporate corruption and greed. *So, as you move up your Money Mountain, and plan for tomorrow by investing today — invest smart, and don't put all your savings in one basket.*

Most young people get caught up in the excitement of the moment. Remember when you were a child, and it was time to open presents? You probably never cared where your parents got the money to buy your birthday or holiday present, you just wanted the presents! Maybe, your mom or dad had to work an extra job to get you the toy you so desperately wanted. Or maybe, your parents had to forego something they needed, just to ensure that you were not disappointed on your birthday. The details of how the present was purchased were not vital information that you needed to know, at the time. You just wanted presents. It did not matter, that after a day or two, the new toy would probably disappear into the closet, hidden from view and forgotten.

As you grow older, you will learn that the yearning for something new and exciting, doesn't really go away. Most people, of all ages, love the anticipation of getting that new and exciting something special, but often, after only a short time, that something special disappears into the garage, or the attic, and becomes nothing more than a very expensive dust catcher. Just remember, there may come a day, when you will wish that you had invested your money, instead of buying more stuff that will eventually need a storage space of its very own.

Money, as you already know, is an instrument to purchase goods and services, but it is also something that can grow very large in value, when invested over time. This is a very important concept that you must understand to climb to the highest peak of your money mountain.

Investing today will create wealth tomorrow.

For example, you decide to open an IRA with a beginning deposit of $3,000. Since you are paid twice each month, you decide to contribute a sum of $125 each pay period, and have it deposited into your IRA account. You earn on average a 10% annual interest rate, compounded semi-monthly.

After 15 years, how much money would you have accumulated in your retirement account? The answer…$117,435.56!

You do not have to be rich, to invest wisely for future prosperity. *A little savings each month can add up to a lot of money, years from now.* Investing for your future is a must throughout your working life. No one knows what the future will bring, but to have a life that is financially sound as you near retirement, you will be required to do good planning today.

When you enter the workforce, your company may offer an opportunity to participate in an employer sponsored retirement plan. This is often a great opportunity to put money away for the future. Your employer may contribute money of their own, by matching a percentage of the money you contribute, in an effort to help you save for your retirement. Over time, these contributions can add up to many thousands of dollars. You should, however, always make certain that you fully understand any benefits that your company may offer, and consult your company's Human Resource department for advice. Most large companies have relationships with stock brokerage companies, who can manage your retirement account during your employment, and offer financial advisors to answer your questions. If you work for a smaller firm that does not offer assistance from a financial advisor, you can consult with a local financial planner and/or a Certified Public Accountant (CPA).

Risk vs. Reward

Any savings plan should look at Risk vs. Reward — *the greater the risk, the greater the return or... the greater the loss.*

There is good risk and bad risk. In the late 1990's, many investors put all their invested capital into Internet stocks. Many people, including brokerage houses, were investing large sums of money in stocks that got a lot of media coverage but little return for shareholders. Many investors thought that Internet stocks, though unproven as an investment, were THE greatest and easiest investment, if you wanted to become rich. Millions of investors were hooked, and some made a lot of money by buying low and selling high... *before the bubble burst.* And when the bubble burst, most found their Internet stocks, which were supposed to be an easy way to retire young and rich, were nothing but a quick way to big losses and, in some cases, a quick way to the poor house.

Not all Internet stocks were bad investments. Some have done well over the years, like Amazon, EBay and others. The problem was that the investors didn't diversify their holdings, to include investments other than Internet stocks.

Investments should always be diversified to include some dependable blue chip stocks, bonds — both domestic and international, and CD's or Money Markets.

No matter how exciting the hype about big money to be made in the Stock Market, you should not invest most of your capital in unproven and explosive new stocks from companies that are currently losing money, and showing no profit dividends to their shareholders. That lack of profitability can last only so long, before the market begins to react negatively.

A wise investor spreads their risk around, so that if the bubble bursts, or the futures market collapses, or real estate is in a freefall, the investor will have a soft landing, and not lose too much of their overall savings. That is the basis of being diversified in your investments.

Greed, and a lust for massive amounts of easy money from your investments, will often result in losses. Most people are not Donald Trump, Bill Gates or Warren Buffett, who have staffs to conduct research, and plenty of money to invest. Most people are not able to spend all their waking hours, researching what their next investment should be. The Trumps, Gates and Buffets of the world are experienced, wealthy experts, who can afford to take great risks, whereas, most people work a regular job and are not savvy investors. Even those "Day Traders", who claim to be Market Pros, often lose on their investments, even though they probably won't admit it.

Do not be tricked, by someone who tells you about a hot stock tip that cannot miss. Most of the time, they are 100% wrong. Remember the old saying "If it sounds too good to be true, it probably is." Third party information about a "hot stock" is too late and usually wrong.

If you simply invest a small portion of your hard earned dollars each month, you will find many years from now, that your money has been working hard for you, and has turned into a lot of cash for your retirement. Every month, put your excess capital, no matter how much or how little, into an investment account such as a no load diversified mutual fund, that is well balanced for your age and risk level.

As you build your career, participate in employer sponsored retirement plans. Start a savings account for purchasing a future home, or car. Have an emergency fund, worth six months of your take home pay, to help you weather any unexpected periods of unemployment.

I cannot stress enough, how quickly money that is invested can grow, as long as it is not placed in poor or unproven investments. Consult financial planners and advisors. Get second and third opinions. They normally will not charge you for an initial visit. Use the Internet to conduct research on financial topics like stocks, bonds, mutual funds, money markets, and CD's. Educate yourself about your investment opportunities. You will become an informed investor and a better investor.

It is your life. It is your money. It is your future. As you climb your money mountain, be a prepared and knowledgeable investor, otherwise you may find that the fall down your mountain is hard, and the climb back up much harder and more uncertain.

"A landlord is more likely to accept less
monthly rent from a tenant who exhibits
a professional appearance and has a good
credit report."

Anonymous

Moving out of the home you grew up in, can be exciting and
also a little scary. More than likely, you probably didn't have
to perform all the chores of daily life while you were living
with your parents. Now that you are out on your own, you
will likely be the one responsible for the cleaning, the cooking,
the clothes washing, the disposal of the garbage, the paying
of the rent or mortgage, of the electric bill and of the cable bill,
too. You'll be the one, who has to pick up the phone and call
for service, when things don't work right. The toilet overflows,

and it's yours to fix. Know any good plumbers? The light fixture in the dining room quits working and a new bulb doesn't fix the problem...*it's on you now.*

Not only, will you be the one who calls for service on the broken parts of your home, you will also be the one paying the bill. Touching up paint, when it shows wear on your walls can get pricey. Purchasing and paying for new bedroom furniture, to replace the furniture you grew up with, can get really pricey.

What about cooking meals for yourself? Odds are you are not the one who slaved night after night over a hot stove to provide food for your family, and you weren't the one who paid for it. And speaking of food, how often in your life have you had to rush off to the grocery store to purchase the coming week's food for the household? Probably, your grocery store visits were primarily to pick up the few items your parents forgot when they were shopping.

Now, it is your time to move out from under your parent's roof, and to begin living in your own home. Since large amounts of money are probably not pouring into your bank account, buying a home is not yet possible, so you decide that you must first rent an apartment or a house.

First, find the area that you would like most to live in, and begin visiting local apartment complexes, until you find the place you would like to call home. What may surprise you is that, in most areas of the country, landlords will ask for a sometimes large deposit, part of which, you may or may not get back when you move out. Landlords may want first month's rent, last month's rent, and a security deposit, which is usually equal to a month's rent. So, if an apartment rents for $750 a month, you will have to come up with $2,250 as "first, last and security" before they will even talk to you about a key. This may not be a simple task, if your bank account is not flowing with money.

Don't get discouraged. When you visit an apartment complex that is of interest to you because of its location, appearance, and almost agreeable monthly rent, there are things that you can do to possibly improve the financial situation. Before you decide on the place where you would most like to live, drive around the complex in the morning, and then again in the evening, as well as during the day on a weekend. This will give you an idea of the amount of available parking in the complex at different times and days, and an idea of how well the complex is lighted at night. By visiting at night you may also see an abundance of available parking spots along with many unlighted apartments, which may indicate a lot of unoccupied units in the development for rent. This may give you cause to look elsewhere, or it might give you a chance to better negotiate with the apartment manager on rent, and the amount of security deposit.

When you first visit the apartment complex, and meet with the property manager, dress professionally. If you look professional, and appear to the property manager like you would be a good tenant in the development, you will have a much better chance of negotiating a lower monthly rent than if you looked and behaved as if you did not belong there. Dress the part. Act professionally and, if you want to live there, do not be afraid to ask for a better monthly rent price. All they can say is no.

The property manager will pull your credit and see if you have been paying you bills on time. *If you have established credit, remember the importance of paying your bills on time each and every month.* The property manager wants to rent to someone that they won't have to track down each month to get their rent payment. They certainly don't want to rent to someone who looks like they'll need to be evicted at some time in the future. If you have good credit established, even if it is relatively new credit, the property manager will feel more comfortable in agreeing to rent you an apartment.

It is incredibly important that you always pay your rent on time each month. This is the time in your financial life when you will be establishing a track record, which will follow you throughout your life. Your rent payment habits will be used later, as an additional credit reference when you begin to pursue purchasing your first home, or if you decide to move to another apartment, or rent a house. It is one important criterion that will be used in evaluating your worthiness for a loan in the future, when you decide the time is right to purchase a home. Most mortgage companies will request a two year history of your rent payments, so they can make sure you always paid your rent on time.

This is extremely important, and you should consider keeping copies of your rent payments in case you ever need to show that they were always paid on time. Pay by check and keep a copy of the cancelled check, or keep an electronic copy if your bank does not return your cancelled checks to you. This will be one way to prove your good payment history, if it is not available from your former landlord, when you are applying for a mortgage. If for some reason, you pay by cash, make certain to get a dated receipt from the property manager to show both the amount of cash received, and that you paid on time.

*"If you think nobody cares if you're alive,
try missing a couple of car payments."*

Earl Wilson

So you want to buy a car? Where do you begin? How much can you afford to spend? Do you pay cash, finance or lease the vehicle? Should you buy new or used? How do you begin your search?

Maybe you've been driving Mom and Dad's car for the last few years gaining experience as a driver and, now that you're working, you think you are ready to purchase a new car of your own. Mom's old car has all those dings on the door, and you have absolutely no idea what she was thinking when she picked that color. It is a vehicle that, though not cool, has been OK, considering it's a free hand me down. It's hard to complain about free transportation, but now you're eager to buy a brand new car of your own.

You've imagined yourself driving some really gorgeous and hot cars you've seen on the road, but you've known in your heart what the thickness of your wallet means. It means that, at this stage in your life, those really hot cars will remain just a dream. Hopefully, you have also been admiring car models that will be more in line with your budget.

Another important decision is new or used. Perhaps a used car with some miles on the odometer and on the engine would be the way to go. Or, maybe your best bet would be a new car, recently delivered to the auto dealer by the manufacturer. Which is best?

A lot of kids today get to go with their family to auto shows, where they enjoy the opportunity to get behind the wheel of the newest cars on the market. Maybe, Mom snapped a picture of you standing in front of one of the coolest concept cars of the future. Standing next to that gorgeous vehicle, you can actually see your reflection in the pristine freshly waxed paint job. It is undoubtedly an exciting feeling to be near the latest, coolest car on the market, dreaming of driving one just like it one day. That day, which seemed so long in the future has arrived, and now it's your turn to choose your very own new car.

Most all of us have opened the door of a brand new vehicle at an auto show, or on a new car lot, and had that rush of excitement. You settle down in the driver's seat, and look through the windshield, while enjoying a whiff of that new car smell, as you get even more comfortable after adjusting the seat to fit your body size. Buying a new car is, for too many people, an emotional purchase, instead of a smart purchase.

The first thing you must learn is that the car you choose must be affordable, and within your budget. You must also know that car dealerships do not exist to help you get the best deal on a car. Everyday, otherwise smart people pay too much for a car because some over eager car salesman and finance manager are willing to take advantage of their lack of knowledge about the car buying process.

Let's say, you've decided which car you really like, and you go to a local dealership to talk about trading in your old car on that new dream car. You don't plan to buy, you just want to talk. Your problems will begin when you walk in the door not knowing what your old car is worth. It is, at some dealerships, the car salesman's job to give you a lot less for your car, than it is really worth, and keep quiet about available discounts.

Your problems will multiply if you believe that you must pay the full manufacturer's list price. Remember automobile dealerships are not in business to teach you how to save money on your purchase, and they are not charitable organizations. So, if you walk in with stars in your eyes and little information other than your credit score, who do you think will be the big winner in this transaction? It won't be the buyer, who is anxious to get in that new car. The big winner in this transaction will be the car salesman and his company.

Everyone is entitled to make a living and earn a fair wage, but some car sellers are willing to cross the line, and take advantage of a customer's lack of knowledge, in a big way. Most car companies and their employees are honest, and try to sell cars at a price that is beneficial to them and the car buyer. But it is your responsibility, as a car buyer, to educate yourself so that when you are buying a new or used vehicle, or selling one, you negotiate the best possible price.

Remember the saying "Knowledge is Power"? Before you begin visiting dealerships to look at cars, do your homework. Research the cars of interest to you. Visit websites like **www. Edmunds.com**, or Kelly Blue Book (**www.kbb.com**). These

websites are a good starting point. They offer a wealth of information to the consumer on car reviews, estimated costs, and
buying advice. Other sites that can help you include **AutoSite.
com**, and **intellichoice.com**. Magazines, like Consumer
Reports (**consumerreports.org**), and government websites,
like the National Highway Traffic Safety Administration at
www.safercar.gov, the Insurance Institute for Highway Safety
at **www.iihs.org**, and the National Highway Traffic Safety
Administration website at **www.nhtsa.dot.gov**, offer consumers a great amount of information on the safety of vehicles.

When you begin your car shopping experience, go to a local
dealership armed with the absolute certainty that, no matter
how much you love the car you are going to take for a spin,
you will NOT buy a car during this first visit. Never buy a car
on impulse. You should have done your research, and made a
list of all the cars that you might possibly be able to afford and
enjoy driving. Then you should test drive each of the cars on
your list. You may just LOVE one of these cars, but remember,
a car salesman spends a lot of time learning how to sell cars,
and the hard sell starts in earnest when they see stars in your
eyes. They are much better at selling cars than most buyers
are at buying a car. So, do not buy a car on your first visit to a
dealership!

It may be hard, as you sit behind the wheel, inhaling that new
car smell, and thinking about how good you would look driving this fabulous car into your driveway. Your friends and
neighbors will be in awe of you. Oh, what a great feeling of
pure desire…Well, it might be a great feeling, but DO NOT
buy the car during the first visit to the car dealership. If you
do, chances are you will be paying too much. Most car sales
people earn a commission when they sell a vehicle. The higher
the price you pay for the car, the greater amount of commission the sales person will earn, and the more the dealer earns.
Before buying, find out if you are really getting a good deal.

The chances of you getting a good deal on your first visit are small. Shopping around at other dealerships and doing your research, is the best chance you have of getting a good deal.

When you start talking price and terms — beware. The deal they offer will sound good, because that is their job, but it may not be the best deal you can get.

One long-term veteran of the auto industry revealed that for every dollar earned above the base profit set by the dealer, the sales person can earn 30% commission on that extra profit. That extra 30% in his paycheck can be a great incentive for a talented sales person. Remember the chapter on negotiation? It will come in handy when you buy a car.

You as the buyer can easily get suckered into paying too much, and you probably don't want to give away hard earn money. Each auto dealership, and each car model on their lot, is going to have different manufacturer incentive program for their staff and for you as the buyer. So, you need to learn, and be prepared for what the dealership's staff is going to do, while trying to get you to purchase a vehicle.

When you first walk into a car dealership a flock of car salespeople place their eyes on you, and look at you as if you are prey. One person will approach you and will try to find out three things as you look at the cars.

1) What kind of monthly payment can you afford to make?

2) Do you have a car to trade?

3) Will you be financing or leasing the vehicle?

The faster the car salesperson discovers the answer to these three questions, the faster they can close the sale. If they get the answers to these important questions quickly, they know they've got you and that you will eventually succumb to your desire to ride home in your new automobile.

The bad news is that you will end up paying more than you should for your new car. Remember: **DO NOT BUY ON YOUR FIRST VISIT.** The name of the game is to save money, and get your car for the best possible price.

The automobile industry teaches their sales staff to sell a car using a sales tool called "The 4-Square System". This method helps to maximize a car's selling price, thus increasing the gross profit for the dealership, and increasing the commission for the salesperson. The 4-Square sales technique utilizes a simple sheet of paper divided into four sections. Once they have a viable buyer, a salesperson simply writes the name of the prospect, along with the car they like and its serial number, at the top of the page. Next, the MSRP (Manufactures Suggested Retail Price) with any added options, destination charges, license, tags and tax are added together, and the amount is written in the top right square. Next, the salesman lists your current vehicles trade-in value in another square. The amount of your down payment and what kind of monthly payment you want, will be placed in the remaining two boxes.

Let's say you can comfortably afford to spend $275 per month on a car payment. The salesperson will respond, "So you want to spend about $300." You answer, "Well, yes, about $300." The salesperson has already gotten you to agree to an additional $25 each month, or $300 per year. See how easy it is, to get someone to move on one of the variables, in the 4-Square sales technique?

So, in one box, you've got the car's total selling price. In another box, you've given information on your preferred monthly payment. In the third box, the trade-in value of your old vehicle is considered as a potential down payment amount. It is in this box, that the dealer can truly maximize their profit, and make you pay a lot more than you should for the car. They likely will start with a low amount in this box.

Once all the boxes are filled, the salesperson has all the information they need to close your sale. You simply have to say, "Yes", and getting you to do that is pretty easy for an experienced sales person. If you hesitate, they will bring in reinforcements, like finance managers, sales managers, and anyone else they need to bring into the negotiation to help close the sale.

Let's say, the salesman wrote in a low number for your trade-in value. That is an area where he has flexibility. Perhaps your trade is worth $4,000, but he only offers you $2,000. He can use that square to hook you. If he started at $2,000, he can bring your trade-in value up to the $4,000 that you wanted for trade-in the first place. He's betting that you will be so happy you just saved $4,000, you simply will not think about negotiating down the car's sticker price. You need to be concerned with all of the 4-Squares!

How do you find out about how much your current car might be worth in trade? Go to Kelly Blue Book (**www.kbb.com**) or **www.edmunds.com** to run a used car search on your vehicle. Find out what the trade-in value is of your old car. Print a copy of the report, and place it in your pocket before you go to a car dealer. Next, go to a car dealer like CarMax, a large national dealer in your area that sells used cars. Ask them to give you an estimate of your car's value. Then, when you go to the new car dealer, ask them to see the current Black Book value for your car. The "Black Book Guide", according to its publisher, National Auto Research, is a weekly guide providing current reports on used car auction results that determine current trade-in values. The dealership is going to want to inspect your car, and that's OK, but you still want to see what the black book recommends as the selling price of your car.

If your car has been in a serious accident, your insurance company probably notified CarFax, which records all collision data supplied by the insurance companies. They notify CarFax using your Vehicle Identification Number (VIN #). This collision reporting service allows any dealer, or consumer, to pull a CarFax and learn the history of a used vehicle. Keep in mind, accidents can affect the value of your trade.

One of the 4-Squares, where you can negotiate for a big savings, is the financing. Financing terms can affect your monthly payment, and can be a big profit area for the dealer.

Let's look at an example, involving the purchase of a new car.

You told the dealer's sales person that you can afford to pay $300 a month. They know how to structure a deal to make the numbers work at that monthly payment. Let's say, the list price for a new car is $24,350. Now, the sales person will ask about your trade-in. You have an old clunker that was a hand me down, and let's say, it is worth $2,500 in trade. When determining the value of your trade, the dealerships' representative will pull out a copy of the current Black Book, and look up your old vehicle. So, now, the salesperson knows what your car is worth in trade, and how much you are willing to pay each month on a payment. The salesman also knows that you have $2,500 down payment towards the new car. All he, or she, has to do is get you somewhere close to a $300 per month payment, and you will be hooked.

When the dealership pulls your credit report and sees your high credit score, thanks to your habit of paying your bills on time, the salesperson says to you, "I can get you in your new car for only $329 a month." You may think to yourself that this is only a few dollars more than you wanted to pay, but you say how about $315. What just happened? You made it easy for the sales rep to close the deal.

The problem is that there are still a lot of unknowns in this business deal. What if the pricing for the car payment is based on a $1,000 trade-in value on your old car, instead of the full $2,500 in trade that was discussed, while you were looking at the Black Book. Auto sales professionals don't like to be real specific on details. They like to talk in generalities about that "affordable" car payment and how much you're going to "love this car". Remember, a salesperson has money to play with, even before considering lowering the cars selling price.

Sometimes a sales person, while pushing that "affordable" payment, will not tell you upfront that the monthly payment is really a 60-month lease, using your old vehicle in trade as the down payment. You are thinking, "Great! I can own my dream car and only pay $315 a month." In reality, you will be driving your dream car, and paying those monthly payments, but you will own nothing. A lease means that you are a renter, not an owner.

So, if at this point, you sign the loan papers, and drive away in your new car, *what will you really have? What did you sign?*

You gave the dealership the $2,500 that your old car was worth, as a down payment. NOT towards a purchase, but towards a lease.

You signed an agreement to lease a $24,350 car for $315 a month for 60 months, or a total of $18,900.

Your warranty period on your new car is for only 36 months, so, for 24 months your car will not be under warranty, and all repairs will come out of your pocket on a car you do not even own.

The lease says in the small print that you are limited to driving only 12,000 miles a year, but you normally drive 15,000 miles a year. So, at the end of the 60-month lease, you have driven an estimated 75,000 miles, but your lease only allowed for 60,000 miles on the car. Since every mile over your allowed amount is is charged 15 cents per mile, at the end of you lease, you still owe another $2,250. In addition, if your car shows wear and tear like dings, dents, or tire wear beyond the allowed amount of your lease, you will owe additional money at the end of the lease for wear and tear.

And, on top of all this bad news, you have nothing of value to trade, since it is a lease, and now, after 60 months, you have to return your old car to the dealership, and buy another car!

This example is not meant to imply that leasing is not ever a good choice. For many people, a lease may work out better than a purchase. Leasing a vehicle can put you into a more expensive vehicle for less money each month, as opposed to buying the same car to own. What is important is to compare the cost of leasing with the cost of buying the car. Negotiate your best selling price, then based upon that price, find out what the monthly lease payment would be for the car at different intervals like 36, 48, and 60-months. Then do the same as if you are purchasing the car to own. Find out the interest rate they are using to calculate the lease and also the purchase. You will often find these two rates different. Then compare the two and total up the payments over the period you plan to lease or own the car.

When you are signing your name to a sales contract, it is really important that you **KNOW** what you are signing. In this case, what you didn't learn from the salesperson could hurt you financially. You need to know the right questions to ask.

DO NOT tell the dealership's staff what you can afford as a monthly payment. Do your homework. Find out what the current interest rates on car loans are in the area where you live. Shop online for the lowest loan rates for new automobiles, or visit local banks, credit unions, and ask car dealers for the rates they offer to their best clients.

When you lease, as well as when you purchase, your credit score factors into your payment. The better your credit the better the rate, or factor, in computing your lease payment.

Always ask the salesperson about any incentives on the car, like rebates, special financing, or lease payments. Whether you lease or purchase, the rebates or incentives can reduce your payments. You must know that they exist, and insure the dealer gives them to you. Remember, you do not have to lease based upon the MSRP price. You can negotiate just like you are purchasing the vehicle.

Also, ask if there are any dealer holdbacks on the vehicle?

...But what's a Dealer Holdback? In your research, you may come across the terms, Dealer Invoice and Manufacturer's Suggested Retail Price (MSRP), for cars and trucks that have been priced with optional equipment on them. The Dealer Invoice is the price the dealer tells you they paid the vehicle's manufacturer for the vehicle. The MSRP is the sticker price, with the price of all options included, which is attached to the window of the vehicle by the manufacturer. **NEVER PAY THE MSRP FOR A VEHICLE, BECAUSE IF YOU DO YOU WILL HAVE PAID TOO MUCH!**

A dealer holdback can save you money, but you will probably not often hear about it from an auto seller. A dealer holdback is money that is allocated, by the car's manufacturer, to the dealer, to help with the financing of the car as it sits on the dealer's lot, waiting for someone to buy it. Usually, the manufacturer pays for this financing cost for the first 90 days that the car is in the dealer's inventory. After this period, the dealer has to pay the financing for each day that the car remains on the lot waiting to be sold.

Often the holdback is a percentage of the cars invoice price, or the Manufacturer's Suggested Retail Price. Many cars can have a holdback allocation to the dealer of up to 3% of MSRP, or Dealer Invoice Price.

Let's look at an example... Say a new car is delivered to a car dealer at an MSRP cost of $28,000. The dealer invoice is at $26,000. If the dealer holdback is 3% of the MSRP, then the invoice price to the dealer is actually $840 less than the $26,000 price, or $25,160.

The longer the car sits on the dealer's lot, the less the holdback value to the dealer. If he sells the car quickly, the holdback is the dealers' to keep. This gives a dealer the ability to advertise to sell a car quickly. The faster the dealer sells the car, the more money the dealer makes.

Now, if the manufacturer is offering rebates on the vehicle you're interested in, then the true invoice price to the dealer is even less. In the example above, if the rebate was $1,500, then the car's cost to the dealer is:

	$26,000 *dealer invoice*
−	$ 1,500 *less rebate*
=	**$24,500**
−	*Less the 3% holdback price to the dealer which will vary*
=	**$23,660 bottom line dealer cost of vehicle**

Always ask the dealer to see the dealer invoice price on the vehicle you are buying. Remember, a good car dealer and sales person will disclose all to you. They want to earn your business. You must remember that knowledge is power, and the more you know, the more they will NOT try to sell you something that you do not need.

Know every vehicle option associated with the car, and its cost on the invoice. A less equipped car will have a lower Dealer Invoice and MSRP, and may appear to be a better deal because of costs. You just have to decide if the car has all the available options on it that you want on your car. Sometimes, when options are grouped together in a "package", they cost less than if they were bought separately. Your research should have identified all available options, and your salesperson can inform you of the availability of the vehicle options. Make sure you are looking at all the options you want on your vehicle, and compare it to the one you're test driving and considering purchasing.

The Dealer Invoice is a starting point in negotiations. If you appear knowledgeable, it is less likely that an overeager car sales person will take advantage of you. Remember to ask the salesperson about any…

- incentives on the car

- special financing

- lease payments

- dealer holdbacks on the vehicle

Hopefully, now you can see why it is so important to know how much the car costs the dealer. That is just one of the reasons why it is so important that you must not buy on the first visit. Gather as much information as possible, so when you go back to the dealer, or price compare at other dealers, you have a good idea how to buy a car, and how to get a good deal. Remember, even though the holdback is not money that the dealer normally gives the buyer, it is still money in their pocket and it reduces the cost of that vehicle to the dealer, and may help a knowledgeable negotiator.

If you have a pretty good idea about how the game works, and you know the true cost to the dealer of the car that you're interested in buying, then you will probably end up buying your new vehicle at a good price.

Purchasing Your First Home

Chapter

17

"Home is an invention on which no one has yet improved."

Ann Douglas

Buying Your First Home

If you have been managing your money well, and saving a little of your take home pay each month, while watching your money grow during the beginning of your career path, then you may have saved enough for a down payment on your first home. There comes a time for most people when they no longer want to help their various landlords become wealthy. Instead, they would prefer to help themselves build a larger financial portfolio. Real Estate ownership is a dream for most Americans, and historically, has been a great long term investment.

In the beginning, most young Americans must rent their first home out of necessity because a rental is all they can afford. Purchasing can be a difficult and expensive challenge. A purchase requires a lot more cash-on-hand than the "First, Last & Security" that a rental requires. However, if you have saved a few dollars each month, you may well be able to afford to purchase your first home.

According to census data, homeownership rates in the United States were at an all time high of 69% in 2006, up 3% since 1980. Millions more Americans can call themselves homeowners today. Homeownership is an American dream for most people and those who are able to join the ranks of Homeowners in America will be those who develop a plan, and then work that plan.

So, let's say you have worked hard climbing each financial step toward your mountain's top, and find yourself perfectly positioned to fulfill your dream of homeownership. Before making that final decision to buy, you need to assess the options associated with owning your first piece of Real Estate. Where do you begin? What do you have to do to realize your dream?

A home will very likely be the largest purchase you will ever make. It is a purchase that will hopefully give you tremendous pride each day as you walk through your front door and cross the threshold into your home. However, before you get to this very exciting step in the home buying process, there are many things that you must consider prior to beginning your new home search. A few of the things you must consider are:

- Where do you want to live?

- How much can you afford to spend?

- How are you going to pay for the home?

- How much money will you need to borrow?

- What are the closing costs on a home purchase?

- Do you need insurance to protect the home from fire, theft and more?

- Do you have to pay property taxes?

- Will you be required to purchase mortgage insurance?

- What is your credit score?

- Have you always paid your rent on time?

- Do you have any emergency savings in the bank?

- Is your current employment secure?

And that is just the beginning…

In the next chapter, we will discuss finding a lender who will help you to obtain the necessary financing for your home and what you should look for in a mortgage. Here we will begin with finding that new home that is just perfect for your needs.

First, your planning process should begin at least six months before you even start to look for a home in the area where you would like to live. Why, you may ask, does this require so much time? Remember when in Chapter 4, we discussed the importance of Understanding Credit? Knowing the ins and outs of real estate is equally as important. Just as there are many benefits to owning real estate, there are also many pitfalls for those who do not know how to protect themselves during the many complex steps of a real estate purchase. A shrewd buyer of real estate comes into the process knowing how the game is played and understanding the important role that a credit score plays as they ascend to their mountain's peak.

Your credit score is the foundation of your financial future. When your credit is good or excellent, companies are more apt to lend you money because they will consider you a worthy credit risk. They believe the chance that you will not pay back your loan is minimized by your excellent credit rating. They consider you a good manager of your money. In the Credit chapter we discussed how even the slightest mistake with your credit, like a late payment to the bank on your credit card bill, can cost you dearly when it comes time to purchase a home. Being, even occasionally, late paying a bill can chop away at your excellent credit rating. The more blemishes you have against your credit, the less likely anyone will want to lend you money.

So, how do you plan to manage your credit situation up until the time you are ready to purchase your first home? Though the importance of maintaining a good credit rating cannot be stressed often enough, there is something that is equally as important. That is how responsibly you maintain your Bank Account. In Chapter 3, I discussed the need to manage your money responsibly and establish a relationship with a bank and its representatives. It is at this time, when you are ready to begin the process of homeownership, that you can call on your relationship with your bank and begin the process of learning how banks, and other mortgage lenders, are going to view you as a credit risk.

It is advisable that the first step in your pursuit of homeownership be to learn about yourself. Prior to beginning your home search, you should have a credit report pulled on yourself. Remember, while you have been building your credit and establishing a credit profile with the banks and credit repositories, you have also been acquiring a credit score from the credit bureaus. This Credit Score is what all the lenders will use to judge whether they should lend you money or not.

Each year you can request one free credit report from America's credit information repositories: Trans Union, Equifax and Experian. You may order you annual free credit report at **www.annualcreditreport.com**. A short time after requesting a copy of your credit report, you will receive your free report, and it will show you exactly what the banks and mortgage lenders see. If you have done your job well, and have maintained good credit, then the banks will more than likely respond favorably when they are determining whether or not to give you a loan.

A new home in the United States in December 2006 averaged $239,700 according to the National Association of Realtors. That is only an average. Some states, like California, have much higher home prices while other states, like Texas, have lower average home prices. But in all cases, you will most likely need to borrow a lot of money from a bank or mortgage lender when purchasing a home. After learning your credit score number, which determines how a bank will view your credit risk, you must decide how much of a payment you can afford to make each month, before you enter into a contract to purchase a new home.

Some of the world's richest men and women, throughout history, have built there fortunes on real estate. History has proven that every successful real estate investor has one thing in common. They purchased their first property, and they had to do the required research to determine where they wanted to buy, and how much real estate they could afford.

Technology has tremendously simplified researching real estate opportunities. Today, you have vast amounts of information readily available 24-hours a day on the Internet, and that may be the best place to begin your research.

REALTOR.COM, the National Association of Realtors consumer website, lists all properties that are for sale and represented by a Realtor® all across America. Listed properties often have pictures, and some even have virtual tours. You can search for listings by criteria that are important to you, such as price, city, amenities, and more. There are other web sites, such as **BYOWNER.COM** and **FSBO.COM,** which list properties being sold by private owners who are not represented by a Licensed Realtor®. Not all licensed real estate agents are Realtors®. Choose to work with real estate agents that are members of the National Association of Realtors because they have the training and professional designation that allows them to use the trademark, Realtor®. You may also find local real estate companies that have offices and websites in the area where you are looking to buy. Often, these websites have links directly to local Multiple Listing Services in your preferred community, which displays all actively listed homes for sale in the area.

If you are going to use a Realtor®, since they tend to be the experts about the communities where they list and sell properties, it is important to select the right real estate agent to help you. There are many part time and full time Real Estate agents that lack the experience to be a lot of help to you. So, as you look for an agent, interview many before you make a choice. Find out who the top buyer agents are in the community where you are looking for a home.

There are, generally speaking, three different kinds of real estate agents. Seller's agents prefer working for the seller's best interests. Buyer's agents prefer working to benefit the buyer, and there are some agents who represent both the buyers and sellers in a real estate transaction.

As a buyer, you are better off finding a buyer's agent who has a thorough knowledge of the Real Estate market in the neighborhood where you wish to live. The sellers' Realtor® works to get the best deal for the seller, but you as the buyer need someone on your side who will work for your best interests. You deserve to have someone working on your behalf that will take the responsibility of helping you to get the lowest price you can on the home you want to purchase.

A buyer's agent usually prefers to work with buyers rather than listing properties for sellers. Whoever you choose as your Realtor®, remember that once you find a home on which you wish to make an offer, the negotiation process begins, and you need an experienced negotiator working to help you.

A good agent will know the price of comparable properties for sale in the community, and should work on your behalf to secure the best price from the seller. A good agent does their homework and investigates the property, the seller and the neighborhood like a detective. Your Realtor® should know what the seller paid for the property, and whether or not there are any personal situations that have contributed to the property going up for sale, such as financial problems, job relocation, and divorce just to name a few.

Your Realtor® should try to uncover the reasons that have caused the seller to want to move, and should know how much the seller owes on the home. Keep in mind that if you have high credit worthiness, are financially stable and are an upwardly mobile buyer, the Realtor® and the seller would be lucky to have you as a buyer for the property. You should also realize that a Realtor® is only going to be paid a sales commission if you purchase and close on a property.

You must also know and remember this... A Real Estate agent is looking to find you a property that you want to purchase because they want their commission. A seller and his agent are looking to sell their property to you because the seller wants out of the property. Neither of these parties should get anything they want until you come to a negotiated price that is good for you.

If you choose a Realtor® who really knows the Real Estate market, they can negotiate on your behalf to get the best possible sales price. It is very easy, as an eager first time home buyer, who is all excited about becoming a homeowner, to overpay for a home if you don't have someone working to get you the best available price.

When you are negotiating price on a piece of real estate, you must remember that just a few thousand dollars difference in the sales price can add many thousands of dollars to your total payments over the life of the loan. Your Realtor® is being paid a lot of money to find you a home and a good Realtor® can be worth every penny that they receive if they are helping you keep your costs down. Educate yourself on the process involved in real estate in your area, and you will have a better chance of finding a Realtor® who will look out for your best interests.

"People are living longer than ever before, a phenomenon undoubtedly made necessary by the 30-year mortgage."

Doug Larson

Financing Your New Home

You will most likely need to borrow a lot of money when purchasing a new home. A bank, mortgage lender, or broker is where you will begin your search for the answers about financing your home. You should already know your credit score, which will give you an idea of how a bank will view you as a credit risk, and you should have an idea about how much of a payment you can afford to make each month on your new home. The financial representative of the bank, or mortgage company, is able to help you answer some of these questions, if you need assistance.

There are several factors that will determine your overall mortgage payment. They include the price you pay for your new home; the amount of money you have for a down payment; your total loan amount; the interest rate you will pay for the money you are borrowing; the insurance you must buy to protect your lenders' investment in the home, as well as your own investment; and, the property taxes on the home. These factors will determine if you can afford the home you want.

The type of financing you choose can affect your home's affordability, and it can have a big influence on the amount of financial risk you assume when purchasing your new home.

Without doubt, that small piece of land with a house on it will be one of the biggest, if not the biggest purchase you will make in your lifetime. And, you deserve to have a comfortable and safe home. Owning a home that we can call our own is one of the reasons we all work so hard each day. However, with homeownership comes responsibility in making sure that you can afford your home. Thus, you must get the right mortgage loan, and know **with certainty** that you can afford the home you decide to purchase.

The mortgage process is quite confusing… *possibly by design*. You need to thoroughly understand the mortgage product (loan type) that you select for your home mortgage.

What I am about to tell you — **your bank, your lender, nor your loan officer will tell you.** If you abide by these simple steps that follow, not only will you save a great deal of money, but you will be a smarter home owner and a smarter investor.

The first thing you must know is that you **NEVER** select the first mortgage lender, or bank, that you talk to regarding the financing of your home. Interview at least three companies. Know that, whichever company you choose as your mortgage holder, they will be lucky to have you as a customer. You may be there to borrow money from them, but they know that you, as a high credit valued customer, can go anywhere to get the money you need to acquire your home. Remember that they need you, and other clients like you, to stay in business. You are doing them a favor by considering them as your financial institution.

When you meet with a loan officer, they will be deciding what loan product and interest rate is best to offer you. No one is going to offer you a free loan, so the first thing to know is that this loan officer is being paid a commission, or some form of compensation, if you select their financial institution as the mortgage holder for your new home. Most often, loan officers, even in a bank, are making an added commission when you select their financial institution for your loan. The higher the rate they charge you for your loan, the more they will be paid, and the more commission they will make. You job is to negotiate for the best mortgage product available to you at the lowest rate.

While exploring various lenders and banks, you may find fluctuations, in interest rates and good faith estimates of closing costs, among different companies. There are many mortgage products that a loan officer could recommend to you, just as there are many companies from which you may choose. You should, however, beware. There will be many potential lenders that may seem good on the surface, but who in the long run could be very bad for you. For instance, a loan officer may recommend a teaser introduction rate that starts off at a very low interest rate and payment, but then suddenly and quickly accelerates the payments to a level that you could not afford on your best day. Certain unscrupulous lenders may even try to sell you a product like this, in order to get you approved for a loan amount larger than you can really afford.

Remember, the larger your loan amount, the more money the loan officer, the bank and the mortgage lender make from your loan. These "teaser rate" products, *often known as Option ARMs (Adjustable Rate Mortgages),* may not be in your best interests. Selecting the wrong product, or the wrong company as your mortgage holder, can too often end up costing you more money than you should be paying, thanks to a bad interest rate and high closing costs. So, take a little time and do your homework.

Let's look at an example. Let's say, you have done a very good job at keeping your credit score high by managing your income and expenses professionally, and paying your bills on time. Your ability to stay on top of your spending should entitle you to the best mortgage rate and terms in the market.

There are literally dozens of mortgage products, which are too numerous to discuss in detail in this book. Therefore, we are going to assume that you will be looking for a 30-year fixed rate mortgage product, which is standard for new home buyers. So far, it may seem easy to you, but remember that nothing in real estate is so easy.

This standard real estate deal appears, on the surface, to be simple. It is a loan product called a 30-year fixed rate loan. That means you will borrow money, and you will repay the original loan amount, plus interest, over a 30-year period. You go to Bank A, and they offer you a 6% loan. Bank B offers you a 6% Loan, and bank C offers you a 5.50% loan. *Which is best?* Your first instinct may be to believe that C is the best deal, because it is the lowest rate.

Now, let's throw in another variable. Bank A charges you a 1 Point fee for the privilege of receiving the loan. Bank B charges you no points, and bank C charges you 2 Points. *Confused?* Most people are.

Let's assume, that in this example, you want to borrow $200,000. With Bank A, you are charged 1 Point, or 1% of the loan amount ($2000), to get a 6% rate. At Bank B, you are given 6% without having to pay points; and at Bank C, you receive a 5.50% rate by paying 2 points ($4000). Confused even more? Look at the figure below.

Loan Amount $200,000

	Bank A	Bank B	Bank C
Interest Rate on a 30-YR Fixed Rate Mortgage	6%	6%	5.50%
Points (Fees)	$2,000.00	0	$4,000.00
Monthly Payment on Loan Amount of $200,000 for 30 Years	$1,199.10	$1,199.10	$1,135.58

What are points in this example? A point is basically money, usually 1% of the loan amount, which you pay to a mortgage company, so they will give you what is called a "discount rate". One point usually equals a one-eighth to one-quarter percent interest rate reduction. So, when you pay a point, that means you should get a better interest rate, than the person who is paying no points at all.

In this example, which is the best deal? We can throw out Bank A right away because, in the example, we paid 1 Point but we are not getting a discounted rate compared to other banks. As you can see in the example, with Bank A, we are paying the same rate and terms as Bank B, but with Bank B there are no Points. We are getting the same rate of 6% and the same payment of $1,199.10 a month. In this case, we must compare Bank B and Bank C. At Bank B, we pay no Points for a 6%, 30-year rate with a payment of $1,199.10 a month. At Bank C, we would pay $4,000, or 2 Discount Point, for a 5.50% rate and a payment of $1,135.58 for 30 years.

Let's say that you plan to live in your new home for three years. As you climb the mountain and gain more wealth, you hope to move to a bigger and more expensive home. If you are only going to live in the home for a short time, it may or may not be worth paying Points to get that lower interest rate. Let's take a look at how many years it will take to recover the $4,000 you would pay in Points for a lower interest rate at Bank C.

At Bank C, you will save $63.52 a month because you will pay $4,000 in discount points, so you can get a 5.50% interest rate. Divide $4,000 by your monthly savings of $63.52, and you'll see that it will take you 63 months to recoup the $4,000 you paid in points at Bank C. If you plan to live in the home for no more than three years, or 36 months, then it does not make sense to pay the Points because it will take more than five years to recover the $4,000 you paid out in Points.

However, there are unknowns, such as tax deductions that you can take on Points paid based on your current income tax bracket, which you should discuss with an accountant before making your final decision. In most cases, however, paying points on a loan that you know will be short term is not a good idea. As you can see from this example, you would have to stay in the home longer than 63 months to make it worth paying the Points to get that lower interest rate. In this example, Bank B with a 6% interest rate and Zero Points is the best option. The payment of points can be very confusing, and often a loan officer will receive a bigger commission on your loan if they can get you to pay points. So, if paying points is something you are considering, contact an accountant to advise you.

Another part of the loan process that you should know about is the fees: a processing fee, an application fee, as well as other miscellaneous fees that some lenders charge. Tell your loan officer that you are shopping for the best product, and best overall closing costs. Always ask for a written loan proposal. If they are not willing to give you what is called a Good Faith

Estimate, or are advising you that it is not necessary to shop other companies, then you should scratch them off your list. If a loan officer is afraid of losing your business because you are comparison shopping, then they are not confident in their products, or they are leaving important information out that you should know. If you can't get complete answers and a Good Faith Estimate, take your business elsewhere.

A mortgage loan is a federally regulated product, and the rate, closing costs and terms of the loan must be given to you in the Good Faith Estimate. Each state has its own closing cost fees, as does each mortgage company, and you have a right to know exactly what your fees will be when you walk into a mortgage closing. You DO NOT want surprises when you sit down at the table to close the sale.

These are the major issues you should consider when selecting a mortgage company. You must select a reputable lender. You must also be aware that even large, well-respected financial institutions can employ unscrupulous or incompetent loan officers. Be ready to walk away any time you feel that you are being squeezed into a loan that could, in the long run, cost you a lot more money than you had planned.

A mortgage is not a simple process, and there are many different types of mortgages available; all the way from first time home buyer programs to adjustable and fixed rate mortgage products. The amount of information you need to know about this process is much greater than what you have read here in this book. Since your first mortgage loan is more than likely several years away for you, you have time to learn more about the process.

When the time comes that you are prepared to get that first mortgage, remember that the first rule is: you must not over spend. The second rule is that you must shop around to get the best mortgage product available to you at the least cost and lowest interest rate.

How do you know if you are overspending? A good rule of thumb is to limit your total monthly mortgage expense (Mortgage Principle Payment plus Interest, Taxes, Homeowner's Association Dues, and Insurance) to no more than 28% of your total monthly gross income. Keeping your mortgage payment within this range will help you to climb a little closer to your mountain's peak. The right mortgage product from the right mortgage lender will help you to save money each month, and those savings can then be invested to grow and grow and grow.

Chapter

Volunteerism

19

"No one has ever become poor by giving."

Anne Frank

Giving Back

As you move up your money mountain and accomplish your goals and dreams, you should consider giving back to your community. Giving to others through volunteerism is an excellent way to offer people who are less fortunate than you, and live within your community, the hope and support that people need in times of hardship.

You might spend a few hours a month at a local homeless shelter feeding the poor. You could join a local, or national, civic or charitable group that focuses on giving. Or you may simply donate money to organizations, like the Red Cross, United Way, or the March of Dimes, just to name a few, that provide services to the needy. Giving back to the community where you live is an important part of your climb up the money mountain. It is also considered by many to be a big part of the success that comes with your accomplishments.

The amount of money and time that you give to help others will, hopefully, change as your financial situation changes. As you grow in your professional career, and as you get older, there will be days when you need the pleasure of seeing a smile on a child's face as they open the only present they will get during the holiday season. The pleasure of that experience will be multiplied if you know you helped to bring that smile to that beautiful little face.

Imagine the strength that a quadriplegic needs, as he or she struggles each and every day just to get out of bed, or to eat a meal. Then imagine what an incredible feeling it would be to know that you helped to improve the quality of life for that person. Believe me when I tell you, helping other people is one of the most rewarding and empowering things you can do in this life. It makes you feel good to know that you have helped another human being. No matter who you are, and no matter what level of financial success you attain, there will always be people less fortunate than yourself who could use a helping hand. Being that helping hand will enrich your life in ways that money never will.

A young boy and his friend used to visit a very old man named Bill in a nursing home once a week. Bill was wheelchair bound because he had lost his legs, in either an accident or during the war. The boys weren't sure, and didn't want to ask. Bill had a wrinkled old face and absolutely no teeth. You might think, just by looking at him, that this old man had nothing to smile about, but every time the boys came to visit, Bill would smile so big, and his wrinkled old face would light up with joy. The boys didn't even know Bill's last name. They didn't know where he came from, or how he got to be in a nursing home, but he was there, and he seemed to have no family. Perhaps he had outlived all his friends and relatives, or maybe they just didn't bother to visit. Regardless of Bill's situation, the boys could see that he was a man who had very little time left to live, and they thought that in whatever time he had left, he deserved to be visited by anyone who could make him smile. The boys thought they were just being friendly and helping someone less fortunate, but they came to realize that the moments they spent with Bill each week made them feel good about themselves. They realized that Bill wasn't the big winner in those visits. They realized that they were the ones who really benefited the most from the time they spent talking to Bill.

People who are less fortunate, and also deserving, will probably not come directly to you and ask for help, but throughout your life, you will come across those who are less fortunate, and are deserving of your help and support. You are the one who will have to decide whether you are the kind of person who will simply walk by and look the other way, or if you are the kind of person who is going to find a way to help those in need.

During your long journey of climbing the peaks of your mountain, and ultimately reaching your mountain's crest, you will need to decide in what ways you can help others. Your journey will probably be spectacular at times, and at other times very difficult. Hopefully, you will be fortunate enough to attain your goals while remembering, there are many in this world that didn't get the lucky breaks, and may never be able to achieve their dreams. Hopefully, you will never have to muster the incredible courage and strength that is required of people who must endure life's nastiest curve balls coming their way. Often, people who have been dealt terrible blows in life exhibit amazing strength and determination to live each day, never complaining about their burdens. It may come to you one day, that helping those in need of a few lucky breaks is a good thing. You will feel all the better for it.

You may donate time to groups like the Kiwanis, National Exchange Clubs, Rotary Clubs, Churches, or Temples. The choice is yours but it is important that you do something. Do not just climb the mountain of your success without taking time to help others. Reaching your mountain's crest will be a great and gratifying personal achievement, but helping others along the way will bring the greatest joy. That moment when you take that final step onto your mountain's peak will be far more fulfilling, and much more exciting, if you know that you have changed lives for the better along the way to the top and beyond.

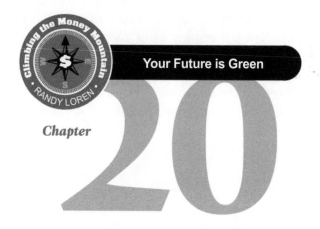

"Every man's obligation is to put back into the world at least the equivalent of what he takes out of it."

Albert Einstein

Your Future is Green

Green is a color that is associated with nature's beauty, as well as with the enormous purchasing power money gives to those who have achieved wealth in life.

Each George Washington dollar bill has very little value by itself, but together, in large quantities, they become hundreds, thousands and millions of dollars, that will buy most anything one dreams. Think of it this way…in an open field a few green trees may go unnoticed, but thousands of trees bunched to-gether become a large never ending "green" forest. We ALL need green!

As you grow in your career, and climb the ladder of success, each step becomes your own personal crusade up your very own Money Mountain. As you ascend the mountain, each step you take in life can now be taken with the knowledge that you are better prepared to avoid the many treacherous paths that will present themselves to you as you move through your life. Hopefully, you will continue to read and learn, so that you will be able to earn more money and accumulate more wealth, so that all your George Washington's can get together and strengthen your portfolio.

If you work smart, honest and hard in life, your portfolio will add up to grow wealth; and the actions of your life will cre-ate a person of wisdom and character. And every person of wisdom and character knows that those green dollars should not only be used for life's comforts, they should also go to ben-efit those who need help in today's world; and those of future generations who come after us in tomorrow's world. We must protect our environment, so that today's green earth will be here tomorrow for people to enjoy.

Back in 1965, billions of years after the planet Earth was cre-ated, the world's population was only 3 billion people. Only 35 years later, in the year 2000, the world's population had doubled to 6 billion people. In 2050, a United Nation's Survey has estimated that the world's population will surpass 9 bil-lion human beings… *each trying to live well, eat and drink well, and vacation well…all together…* right here on our one and only small planet, Earth.

In 1900, a person's lifespan in the United States was a mere 47.3 years. By 1970, with major advancements in medicine, sanitation, cleaner water, improved working conditions and a better standard of living, life expectancy grew to 70.8 years in the United States. In 2004, a person's life expectancy was 77.5 years. It is estimated that by 2050 the life expectancy in the United States will be as high as 87.5 years, and the population of the United States will be around 392 million. This amounts to a growth rate of over 30% from today's population of 300 million.

As the world's population continues to grow, and the standard of living increases around the globe, there will be an increasing demand for, and use of, the Earth's resources. According to the Environmental Protection Agency, the average person in America produces 4.5 pounds of trash a day. With human life expectancy increasing globally, it is very likely that you will live a long life, and will use many of the resources provided by Mother Earth. During your lifetime, both renewable and non-renewable resources will be harvested from the Earth, and used to create products like glass and plastic bottles that will then be used, and discarded, by you every day. That sounds like sort of a good thing, until you realize that these used resources, that YOU use up today, will then create a mountain of waste that will live on in landfills for possibly thousands of years. Multiply that by 392 million Americans in 2050, and you've got a LOT of waste.

As you plan for your financial future, it is important that you do your individual part to ensure that the world you leave behind is at least as good, if not better, than the world you grew up in. Balancing the green of money with the green of nature is your responsibility, and the responsibility of everyone who uses their wealth to purchase products that were made from nature's raw materials...*products that will eventually end up as waste in a land fill.*

When you consider this waste, and take into account the increased longevity of the American people, more than ever before, you need to develop, and implement, a comprehensive personal financial plan. Your plan for the future should ensure that you have enough savings to last through your lifetime, and the lives of your loved ones. It should also take into consideration how a changing environment can affect you, and how you can affect a changing environment.

There has been much debate in academic and political circles in recent years about global warming. Some individuals will argue that global warming is just a hoax perpetrated by those who say they want only to save the planet, but who will somehow profit from this misinformation. Then there are individuals who are convinced that global warming exists and we are in real danger, as we quickly approach a tipping point from which we will not recover if there is no action by human beings to correct global warming. Most scientists, however, are unanimous in their belief that global warming really exists, and it is NOT just an event of a natural ecological cycle; though, there are some scientists who disagree. President George W. Bush said, while traveling to Scotland in 2005 for the summit of the Group of Eight industrialized nations, "I recognize the surface of the earth is warmer and that an increase in greenhouse gases caused by humans is contributing to the problem."

Global Warming is defined as a gradual increase in the earth's surface temperature. An increase in the Earth's temperature brings more potentially fierce storms and hurricanes, like Hurricane Katrina in 2004 that almost completely destroyed New Orleans and the Gulf Coast. If Global Warming is real, it is anticipated by many that a small country in the Pacific Ocean named Kiribati, which is made up of 33 islands, will be completely submerged and uninhabitable within 50 years.

This book is not intended to debate global warming. However, like your right to vote, gaining information on strategic subjects of interest, like global warming, can have a profound impact on you, your family and many others. And, yes, it can have a tremendous impact on your personal and your financial well being. It is always important that you become knowledgeable on present day issues, and then use that valuable information to decide for yourself if these issues will be relevant and important to your life. Analyze the information and decide how it might affect you, your loved ones and others. Knowledge is power, and if you gain the knowledge, you will grow and prosper, and become a better person for all your efforts.

Now, let's look at how the environment may affect you, your income and your life.

We can all agree that the earth has limited resources. For thousands of years, before the industrial age, man used very little of the raw materials available on the Earth. The population then was far less than it is today, and the needs of people were much simpler.

As history has shown, the industrial age of the late 19th and early 20th century was only the beginning of a wave of inventions that created more products, and more opportunity for wealth creation, than ever in the history of mankind. At the same time, it was the beginning of the race for human beings to use up the earth's resources at an alarming rate. As more and more products were invented, and the world's population grew, the resources of the earth were being used up faster and faster. The Earth's renewable resources like trees could be replanted. Nature itself could replenish some of the world's resources on its own. But those non-renewable resources… *those were simply lost to manufacturing forever.*

Basic economic theory states that, as demand for a non-renewable product like fossil fuels (coal, petroleum, and natural gas) increases and supply decreases, prices will rise. If there are more and more people on our planet, they will consume the earth's resources faster and faster. If we don't find ways to replenish or conserve their use, or find alternative sources that are more environmentally friendly, then the resources will simply be lost forever. And in this process, a lot of people will rake in huge amounts of cash while the vast majority of people struggle just to get a little of the dwindling commodity.

The planet's rain forests are continuously logged to meet the world's demand for paper, housing, and exotic woods. If the trees are not replaced, planetary climates can change and many of nature's unique animals will be lost to extinction. In fact, it is estimated that 2 out of every 5 of earth's living animals are in danger of extinction as a result of deforestation. Trees clean our air when they absorb carbon dioxide and release oxygen back into the atmosphere, so that we all can breathe. Forests provide photosynthesis that gives life to all living things, and forests provide shelter and a home to nature's animal life.

Global warming is believed to be caused by green house gases which can be created by natural occurrences, such as water vapor, carbon dioxide, methane, nitrous oxide and ozone. The creators of the greenhouse gases that cause the most damage to our planet's environment, however, are humans. Human beings demand an ever increasing amount of energy for our chosen mode of transportation, and for our creature comforts. For example, in 1900 there were approximately 8,000 vehicles in use worldwide. The vast majority of people got to where they wanted to go on foot, on a train, a boat, a bicycle, or on horseback.

According to *Ward's Auto Vehicle Facts and Figures*, more than 671 million cars and trucks were in use worldwide in 1996. World Book Encyclopedia estimates that by 2030, there will be over 1.2 billion cars on Earth. The United States, today, produces approximately 25% of the global carbon dioxide emissions in the world by burning fossil fuels, the vast majority of which comes from our dependence on automobiles.

In February 2007, the United Nations issued an Intergovernmental Climate Change Report stating, "Warming of the climate system is unequivocal." The cause they say is human activities that have increased carbon dioxide in the atmosphere. This carbon dioxide causes solar heat, that otherwise would have radiated away, to remain in the atmosphere. *So, does global warming exist?* You must decide, but one thing is certain…we can, as individuals and members of the exclusive club of the 6 billion people on Earth, do our part to help reduce the high levels of carbon dioxide in our atmosphere, and live a little more energy efficient life.

So, how does living an earth friendly life affect your climb up the money mountain? Simply put, if you do not take action to help the world's population become more green and eco-friendly, not only will your pocketbook be affected negatively by increasing costs of energy but, many of the world's beautiful green landscapes and unique animals of the world may be lost forever.

Here are some of the small things that you can do to live a more eco-friendly life. You will save money, and it will make you feel good to know that you are part of the solution, instead of part of the problem.

- Consider more fuel efficient cars and carpool when possible.

- Recycle plastics, glass, aluminum cans, newspapers, and any-and-everything your community collects to recycle. A 4-foot high stack of papers is equal to one fir tree. Recycling will save millions of trees a year. A plastic container takes 1,000 years to degrade in a land fill. Throw it away and *it will take 40 generations to degrade in that landfill.* One person on average uses 15,334 plastic bottles and 26,408 aluminum cans in their life. *Multiply that by 9 billion!*

- Change the light bulbs in your home to compact

fluorescent light bulbs which use much less energy but still provides the same amount of light as a regular bulb. Initial costs are more, but long term, the savings are worth it.

- Unplug appliances, televisions, computers and other electronic items when not in use. Even though these appliances are not turned on, they will often still consume a lot of energy when left plugged into an outlet. Consider using a smart power strip that shuts off the power to several items that you do not need, while keeping the power on to the items that are needed.

- Use reusable cloth grocery bags that can be washed and reused, instead of the 380 store plastic bags that are used by an individual, on average, each year. Currently only 3% of plastic bags are recycled.

- When washing your clothes, use warm and cold water rather than hot water. Never run a dishwasher until it is filled, and always use earth friendly detergents.

- When brushing your teeth, turn off the tap while you are brushing, and you will save up to 8 gallons of water per day.

- Program the thermostat, to change temperatures when you are not in the house, to save energy consumption.

- Cut back your shower time, even by one minute. This will save a great deal of water waste over time. Use a shower head that is more environmentally friendly.

Your successful climb up your money mountain will give you many opportunities to choose what kind of person you want to become. As you are reaching the pinnacle of your success, you can use your wealth and knowledge to help your family, your world, your country, and those less fortunate than yourself. Or you can think only of yourself.

You may be one of the smart ones, who are successful and lucky, as you proceed boldly into the future. There will also be many, who are not. They may not have learned in their life:

- How important getting a solid education is to success.

- How important proper budgeting and money management is to long term financial independence.

- How important protecting your personal identity from theft has become in the Internet Age.

- How important good credit is to your long term success, and the resulting savings of lower interest rates that you will pay on car purchases, mortgage loans, and credit cards, as well as your overall financial well being.

- How important is it to negotiate for almost anything you purchase, so you can save money.

- How important it is to continue learning and expanding your skills throughout your career, by reading newspapers, trade journals, magazines and searching the Internet, so that you can constantly improve your abilities and knowledge level regarding your career, and your world.

- How important it is to learn to invest wisely, instead of recklessly.

- How important it is to find the balance between risk and rewards.

- How important it is to save a little each day, so that your savings can become a lot of money in the future.

- How important it is to learn about the issues that affect you locally, nationally, and globally, so you can be a well informed voter and citizen.

- How important it is to volunteer, and offer your time to a national organization, a local group or an individual, so that you can make a life, other than just your own, a little bit better. *And…*

You must balance the green of money with the green of nature. **Green = Green**.

But one thing is certain. You must take care of the environment you live in today, so that your children, great grandchildren, and your great, great grandchildren can inherit a world that is inhabitable, beautiful and green, just like the one you have known in your life.

You are the only one who can decide what kind of life you will choose to live, and what kind of world you choose to leave behind. It is your mountain, and the journey to the top can be a great adventure with achievements beyond your imagination. Your goals and accomplishments can be personally and professionally rewarding. It is your time to make your mark on history. ***One person can make a difference*** and that person can be you. Enjoy your life and all the good that can come to you, as you climb your money mountain to its peak, and beyond.

About the Author

Randy Loren is a sought after motivational speaker and President of Financial Nation, Inc. He has been the recipient of many awards, and has donated much of his time to causes that help children and young adults to lead better lives. He has been a consultant to Loren-Snyder Marketing, a family owned  company, which developed the Martha Stewart Brand for Kmart. He received his Bachelor of Arts degree in Marketing from Michigan State University, and his MBA from Nova Southeastern University. Mr. Loren is Certified in Identity Theft Risk Management (CITRMS) and is a Certified Credit Report Reviewer (CCRR).

Your Personal Checklist
to Your Mountain's Peak

❑ Stay in school. Get as much education as you can, and always improve on your skills by reading newspapers, magazines, trade journals, and attending seminars.

❑ The more education you complete, the more income you will earn.

❑ Higher learning, like going to College should be a great and rewarding experience. Study hard in school and let this period of learning be a catalyst to helping you to achieve your career aspirations and dreams.

❑ Find a mentor to help you learn and grow in your profession.

❑ Build a relationship with a bank by opening a checking account and properly manage the money you deposit and withdrawal from the bank. Find a bank that has little or no fees for opening and maintaining an account.

❑ Never overdraft your bank checking account. Always write the check number, who the check was payable too, and the amount of the check in your check registry. Balance your checkbook when you receive your bank statement.

❑ Never be late when paying your bills. PAY YOUR BILLS ON TIME, AND NEVER BUY WHAT YOU CANNOT AFFORD.

❑ Set short and long term goals and write them down on paper for future reference.

Climbing the Money Mountain Worksheet

❑ Understand how different countries around the world and their economies can affect you career. Do these countries provide products or services similar to what you provide, and can they impact your job and future career mobility.

❑ Always be ethical and professional in your life and career.

❑ Register to vote….Learn the local and national issues and cast your vote.

❑ Watch out for Identity Theft. Protect your personal information at all times.

❑ Do not give out your passwords. Constantly change them.

❑ Be careful what information you provide on websites like, MySpace.com, Facebook.com and others. Do not put pictures or write comments that are inappropriate that others can view online that could affect how people think of you. Remember future bosses and clients may see these pictures and it can potentially affect your career.

❑ You can use your negotiation skills to save money on many products and services. You can also negotiate your salary and salary increases. Prepare by doing research and having supportive information in hand that can be used to help you negotiate a better deal.

❑ Negotiate a win-win situation between you and the person whom you are negotiating.

❑ Establish a Personal Budget that is realistic and that you can maintain. Do not spend more then you make.

Climbing the Money Mountain Worksheet

❑ Be a smart Investor and not one who overacts to the latest gimmick. Invest wisely and consistently throughout your life and watch your money mountain grow. Evaluate risk and reward. Do not invest what you cannot afford to lose.

❑ When Renting…Look professional and know the rents in the area that you are looking to live when meeting with a potential landlord. Drive around at different times of the day in the area you are looking to rent. Negotiate the best rent rate you can as the landlord would be lucky to have you.

❑ Research all car prices online before shopping at an auto dealership. If financing, know your finance options prior to looking for a car. Also find out what kind of monthly payment and how many payments you can expect on a new or used car purchase. NEVER purchase a car on your first visit to an auto dealership.

❑ When buying Real Estate, investigate the area you plan to move. If using a Realtor, select one who has the experience and knowledge in the market area where you want to buy.

❑ Begin planning six months in advance when buying a home to review your credit and financial situation. Know what your mortgage and other home costs like electric will run you prior to beginning your search.

❑ Visit once a year www.annualcreditreport.com for your free credit report.

❑ Shop around for the best mortgage product. Fixed rates are normally the best. Make certain that you compare Good Faith Estimates when researching mortgage companies. Get at least three written mortgage Good Faith Estimates from various mortgage companies or banks, so that you can compare fees and closing costs.

Climbing the Money Mountain Worksheet

❑ Volunteer your time to help others in your community. You will feel good about yourself and at the same time help those less fortunate.

❑ Know how you can help your environment by making small changes in your life, such as recycling, and using more energy efficient lighting. Implement these and more eco-friendly changes as they will help you save money and help protect our Earth for future generations to enjoy.

Personal Goals

SHORT TERM GOALS ~ 1 Year or Less to Accomplish

1. _____
   _____

2. _____
   _____

3. _____
   _____

4. _____
   _____

5. _____
   _____

LONG TERM GOALS ~ 1 to 5 Years to Accomplish

1. _____
   _____

2. _____
   _____

3. _____
   _____

4. _____
   _____

5. _____
   _____